Dispelling Twelve Myths about the Gospel: "Lessons in the Book of Galatians"

© By Dr. Randall D. Smith

These volumes were prepared with students and teachers of the Bible in mind. The series is taken from the actual teaching notes of Dr. Smith as he teaches through all of the Bible each year at Great Commission Bible Institute in Sebring, Florida.

Dispelling Twelve Myths about the Gospel Lessons in Galatians

Each lesson dispels myths, but also offers the key truth principle of the passage:

Lesson One: Galatians 1:1-24 "Myths One, Two, and Three"

Key Principle: The Gospel is how God offers a restored relationship with man based solely on trust in the full payment for sin in Jesus Christ – a payment effective to reconcile the world to God and each other.

Lesson Two: Galatians 2:1-21 "Myths Four and Five"

Key Principle: The gospel teaches that we don't earn a relationship with God through works (because it is a gift given to the undeserving) but we do offer God our lives and seek to obey Him in our walk now that we have been purchased by Him.

Lesson Three: Galatians 3:1-29 "Myths Six and Seven"

Key Principle: God the Father has a permanent irrevocable call to Israel that is entirely separate from the call of the Savior to His church.

Lesson Four: Galatians 4:1-31 "Myths Eight and Nine"

Key Principle: God kept in place unique markers for the Jewish people (because He has a future plan for them) that the church around the world need not be concerned about adopting, no matter what pressure they receive to do so.

Lesson Five: Galatians 5:1-13 "Myth Ten"

Key Principle: True freedom is found in intimate attachment to God initiated by faith in Christ alone, and lived out by careful diligence in following God's Spirit.

Lesson Six: Galatians 5:14-26 "Myth Eleven"

Key Principle: The mature believer learns to let the empowering of the Spirit bear the fruit of the Spirit. He isn't interested in trying to do what doesn't honor the Savior in the name of freedom.

Lesson Seven: Galatians 6:1-18 "Myth Twelve"

Key Principle: When the family comes together, we must face the fact that some issues (and some people!) need to be dealt with in very specific ways.

Table of Contents

Dispelling Myths about the Gospel: Lessons in Galatians

Lesson One: Galatians 1:1-24
"Myths One, Two, and Three"

Very few movies can begin in the middle of the story, but *Star Wars* did just that. I was in High School when the "Jedi knights" were first heard of on our planet. The words "A long time ago in a galaxy far, far away..." entered vernacular speech in a new series of movies that has seemingly refused to die. What was really curious was the idea of starting on Episode IV: A New Hope in 1977, and then working forward for a few years in the storyline. After a hiatus, the film makers came back to the series decades later and offered a new set of prequels (a word I had never heard before these films), ending in the now proposed final installment in 2015. The galaxy is big, but this story has really taken a LONG TIME to tell... Many of the movie goers to the last episode weren't even born when the first episode came out!!

I didn't come to criticize the Sci-fi film series. Rather, I want you to think about a real message from far, far away. From the edge of space, far beyond our galaxy a message has come. It is real, reliable, exciting and an unbelievably helpful message. It isn't the stuff of science fiction but a communication that will make more difference to you than an announcement that we have found sentient life on Mars.

The message I am speaking of arrived two thousand years ago, and though many in the world have desperately tried to silence it, mar its credibility, and indict its authenticity – it is a message that has changed literally billions of lives. It is the message of the Gospel, and it is a message alive and moving out, shattering darkness with its light. It is piercing the armor of the rebellious men with the arrows of truth – and it is a threat to them. For that reason, it is also a message under attack. It is a message that must be held at the center of the church and recited by each generation of Christians. It is a message easily burdened with mythology, and only carefully cleansed by re-examination of the ancient texts that revealed its truth to us.

That is what this series is designed to do. We will look, line by line, at one of the most complex arguments about God's acceptance that has ever been penned. It will take time, and it will cover some things very familiar – but it MUST be re-examined. Some of it may even surprise you! As we start out examination, let's begin with a definition of the Gospel derived from the *Bible*, and use it as our key principle.

Key Principle: The Gospel is how God offers a restored relationship with man based solely on trust in the full payment for sin in Jesus Christ – a payment effective to reconcile the world to God and each other.

Because of the importance of the message, we need to be sure we have not allowed the message to be stained with modern popular mythology. We need to answer some specific myths that some have tried to stick to the message as far back as the first century – and some are trying even today. What is surprising is how little has changed in the attack of false ideas over the last twenty-one centuries! Let's filter out mythological stains and see the Gospel as it was intended to be!

Myth 1: Afterlife Insurance - It's all about Heaven! The Gospel isn't about this world, but the next.

We have all heard the saying: "So heavenly minded they are no earthly good." Often that saying was offered on behalf of one that seemed disengaged. Now we may say it but mean something different – saying those who DISENGAGE GOD'S WILL from daily life, and emphasize the Gospel's provision of "afterlife insurance". Many mistakenly emphasize the afterlife in relation to the Gospel, but that is understandable. After all, it is no small thing to have one's eternal destiny changed by means of accepting Christ. At the same time, an over emphasis on the afterlife can lead to a Gospel that is ineffective this side of Heaven. Listen to the letter in Galatians 1:

Galatians 1:1: Paul, an apostle (not [sent] from men nor through the agency of man, but through Jesus Christ and God the Father, Who raised Him from the dead), 2 and all the brethren who are with me, To the churches of Galatia: 3 Grace to you and peace from God our Father and the Lord Jesus Christ, 4 Who gave Himself for our sins so that He might rescue us from this present evil age, according to the will of our God and Father, 5 to Whom [be] the glory forevermore. Amen.

Before we can explore his presentation of truth of the Gospel, we need to meet the author and review his expertise. Without a 'book jacket" the biblical author could only introduce himself inside the letter, and then launch into the burden of his heart for the recipients. Paul opened the letter with a different twist than his normal self-introduction. There was a purpose behind each statement in the opening, and in this letter he made clear that **he was three things:**

First, An ambassador of God: (*apostello*, cp. 1:1) Paul wasn't writing simply because he was disappointed in the state of affairs among the believers in Galatia – though he was. He wrote on behalf of another – God Himself. If that wasn't so, nothing in the letter truly matters. Truth of Scripture is God's truth dispensed through the human quill. These aren't the collections of Paul's sage advice, or management tips based on his experience. These are words of one of the "holy men moved of God's Spirit" (2 Peter 1:21) to offer direction from God's Spirit.

This understanding is critical for the presentation of everything we will examine over the next six studies in this letter. Either these are God's carefully exposed truths, or they are the words of a man who gave "his best shot" at explaining truth as he saw it. Churches divide exactly on this issue. **We believe and teach without apology that Paul was what he claimed to be – an Apostle, an ambassador.** When he wrote things that challenge our culture, we cannot simply dismiss them as "bad ideas" as some who claims Jesus today readily do. Paul claims to be speaking for God in the way an ambassador of our country speaks for our President. In that way, Paul's words are God's Words.

Second, Appointed without human agency directly by Jesus and the Father: (1:1). Paul claimed in the letter that he was not "voted in" to his position by a council or a committee. **He was appointed by God, and specifically engaged by the risen Jesus Himself.** These words are also chosen carefully, because the message of this letter is going to challenge assumptions. At some point in the reading of the letter, any first century reader was going to be challenged by the direct tone and unshakeable presentation of Paul. The writer wanted to make one thing clear: He was speaking from the highest authority, utterly certain of the Savior's true wish in regards to the issues plaguing the group of believing recipients.

Third, In harmony with his brothers: (1:2a). Paul emphasized that he was not writing from a faction that stood in opposition to all others. He was not some subversive dissident; he was standing with the main stream. The fact that many agreed with him and that he walked in harmony was not the proving factor to Paul – his relationship with Jesus and commission from Him was. Why mention it then? Because it is important sometimes to show that when you are challenging assumptions you are doing it from a body of wise counsel, and not taking shots on your own. The phrase: "all the brethren who are with me" implied that Paul was writing with the knowledge of others, and in harmony with their view as well.

Let's also be clear about the **recipients of the original letter**, because it will answer some queries as to why he chose to say certain things the way he did. **Paul was clearly writing to BELIEVERS.** This letter isn't designed to simply expose the way to FIND GOD for those who do not know Him, it is a careful explanation of how they found Him already, and why their pull from the Gospel is a pull from the truth (1:2b-3). They are IN the churches of Galatia, not in the fields to be reached – but even they were struggling to see the truth of what the Gospel means.

Here is the point: **Even the church can struggle to truly grasp the truths they have already proclaimed. False teachers abound – some proclaiming thoughts in ignorance and causing confusion, and others deliberately enticing people into compromise, empowered by God's enemy**.

- Because someone claims to be a Christian doesn't mean he is.
- Because someone claims to be telling the truth doesn't mean he is.
- Because someone mentions Bible verses in their message doesn't mean they are speaking from the truth of those passages.

Paul largely addressed this writing to people who knew him. He wrote to people who followed his career well enough to know his honesty, integrity, authenticity and sacrifice for the truth.

By verse four (1:4), Paul arrives at the first truth concerning the Gospel that many of us observe has been mishandled, creating a mythology about salvation.

Paul wrote in *Galatians 1:4 ...Who gave Himself for our sins so that He might rescue us from this present evil age, according to the will of our God and Father...*

With those words, Paul makes clear that those who respond in faith to the Gospel have more than received a change in their eternal destiny; they have allowed the Spirit of God to change their lives in their present Earth-walk. The Gospel doesn't engage us at physical death; it is the device that replaces our spiritual death.

In the Bible, the word "death" is used of different things. Its primary meaning is the cutting off the flow of spiritual life – the severing of the umbilical cord with God – that happened at "The Fall" in the Garden of Eden. The *Bible* tells the story of our progenitor, Adam, and his wife, Eve, and their rebellion. In the earliest chapters of the Genesis (2 and 3) we read of the sentence of "death" that passed immediately upon them when they rebelled. That spiritual disconnection is used of "death," and the physical death that we recall at a graveside is a reflection of that spiritual one. To the Ephesians (in the beginning of chapter two), Paul made clear that believers in Christ "were dead, but are now made alive." In that sense, the *Bible*'s primary use of death (in the theological sense) is not about the body, but about the spirit.

Let me say it another way: **Before you asked Jesus to enter your life in a deliberate act of surrender, the *Bible* says you were "dead" in relationship to God**. That doesn't mean that you didn't believe that God existed – it means that His existence had little to do with how you lived your life, made your choices or declared your personal values. You knew God as I know celebrities from the movies. We KNOW they exist, but we don't have a relationship with them that changes how we do what we do. The *Bible* calls a man or woman that may have a vague notion of a God in Heaven but has not entered a deliberate relationship with Him "dead" to God. They walk and talk in this life, but they are spiritually "dead." The interesting thing is that biblically, this kind of "death" precedes "life." The decision to surrender one's heart to Jesus brings LIFE; the choice to live life on one's own is "death."

In the opening of the letter, Paul made clear that NEW SPIRITUAL LIFE BEGINS NOW, as our walk with Jesus was to "rescue us" from this age. You may not know it, but the Bible says that you are in peril right now. The current of this age is strongly pulling you in a direction toward destruction. The self-made men and women of our day, who are proudly attempting to create a morality without God, are filling your ears with anti-surrender, anti-God rhetoric. They may not be shouting "We HATE God" (though some certainly are, but they are making clear they neither NEED HIM nor DESIRE THE MORAL CONSTRAINTS that come from a relationship with One Who created us, and will hold us to account of His directions.

The Gospel is a deliberate surrender to the One Who made us. It is NOT simply a "get out of Hell free" card – it is the response to God's goodness in receiving the gift of the Savior's full payment for salvation and beginning a deliberate and conscious relationship with God in Christ. The Gospel changes my decision making process NOW, not just my eternal destiny THEN. It is a Gospel that changes what I laugh at, how I maintain my body, what priority I give to knowing His Word, and how I engage people. It is a Gospel to rescue me from the drowning currents of self will and arrogance all around me. It is clutching the hand of a God that grabbed me when I wasn't even sure I was drowning in this life. The Gospel isn't just "AFTERLIFE INSURANCE"; it is the CHANGE AGENT of my life now, rescuing me from godless thinking and selfish decision- making.

Myth 2: Fuzzy - The message is very subjective! You can't really tell if people are preaching it properly.

Another myth bandied about in circles that claim to be Christian is that the Gospel is a fuzzy body of information – that you cannot tell if someone is truly preaching and teaching it or not. Paul wrote:

Galatians 1:6 I am amazed that you are so quickly deserting Him who called you by the grace of Christ, for a different gospel; 7 which is [really] not another; only there are some who are disturbing you and want to distort the gospel of Christ. 8 But even if we, or an angel from heaven, should preach to you a gospel contrary to what we have preached to you, he is to be

Dispelling Myths about the Gospel: Lessons in Galatians

accursed! 9 As we have said before, so I say again now, if any man is preaching to you a gospel contrary to what you received, he is to be accursed! 10 For am I now seeking the favor of men, or of God? Or am I striving to please men? If I were still trying to please men, I would not be a bond-servant of Christ.

Paul's statement is straightforward – I preached a Gospel that you MUST NOT exchange, amend, alter, or confuse. It was truth then, and it is truth NOW. You cannot weave new requirements INTO THE GOSPEL nor can you extract components of it. The stature of the one who would oppose it doesn't matter – you must stick to what you were told. Some men will adjust the message to make it more palatable, but they serve men and not Christ. They don't want to take a stand on the truth, so they ease off the specifics.

When Paul explained the Gospel, he specified what he was talking about.

The term gospel is found ninety-nine times in the NASB and is normally the translation of the Greek noun *euangelion* (which occurs 76 times). The others are simply translated "good news." The verb form of the word is used another 54 times as *euangelizo*, which means, "to announce good news." These words grow from the noun *angelos*, or "a messenger." The point is that such extensive use of the word reminds us that the main message of the church is not sinfulness, nor condemnation, but GOOD NEWS of reconciliation made possible.A careful study of the gospel will yield some of its chief components that were repeated many times in Scripture. The gospel is the message of good news that God has provided a way of salvation for men through the gift of Jesus' payment to the world. Jesus died as a sacrifice for sin, overcame death, walked out of the tomb, and now offers reconciliation to God to all who will accept the payment He made on their behalf. It is by grace – an undeserved gift of God, and it is through faith – energized by belief that what God says is true is true. It cannot be attained by any form of penance or work of self-improvement. It opens the door to a permanently reconciled relationship to God, and offers an eventual restoration of man to all Creation.

The apostle offers **Ten Facts concerning the Gospel of Jesus Christ** (1 Corinthians 15:1-11) that caused the formation of a body of "believers."

1 Corinthians 15:1: Now I make known to you, brethren, the gospel which I preached to you, which also you received, in which also you stand, 2 by which also you are saved, if you hold fast the word which I preached to you, unless you believed in vain. 15:3 For I delivered to you as of first importance what I also received, that Christ died for our sins according to the Scriptures, 4 and that He was buried, and that He was raised on the third day according to the Scriptures, 5 and that He appeared to Cephas, then to the twelve. 6 After that He appeared to more than five hundred brethren at one time, most of whom remain until now, but some have fallen asleep; 7 then He appeared to James, then to all the apostles; 8 and last of all, as to one untimely born, He appeared to me also. 9 For I am the least of the apostles, and not fit to be called an apostle, because I persecuted the church of God. 10 But by the grace of God I am what I am, and His grace toward me did not prove vain; but I labored even more than all of them, yet not I, but the grace of God with me. 11 Whether then [it was] I or they, so we preach and so you believed.
Look closely at the specifics from the verses above:

First, It was brought to them in content and ANNOUNCED (*euangellion* – cp.1). It is found in a good message that can be verbally communicated. The gospel isn't a harsh message that brings condemnation – but a liberating message of full payment. We aren't sharing RULES with people – we are declaring their bondage ended!

Second, The hearer had to **CHOOSE** to "take it along with them" ("receive" is the term *paralambano* – 1b). It was an active reception. The gospel requires response and grasping. It is an active and deliberate process – not a passive one. No one gets to Heaven by accident, stumbling in the pearly gate. They must decide to receive the message.

Third, The choice caused the recipient to "take their stand" or "fix their hold" on it ("stand" is the term *histemi* – 1b). It changed the recipient in future action. Having decided on the veracity of the message, they must cling to that message. The life perspective changed, they are not fickle – but cling to the Cross.

Fourth, The choice to receive the announcement and fix hold on it saves the recipient ("save" is *sozo* – from "to rescue or cure" – v.2a). If sin is the sickness, the gospel is the cure. One must understand that without the gospel a man or woman is not simply "impaired" but LOST. In John 14:6 – "Jesus said to him, "I am the way, and the truth, and the life; no one comes to the Father but through Me." The issue of SAVED and LOST is technically separation from the Father in Heaven.

Fifth, The salvific effect occurs only for those who possess the Gospel (the terms "hold fast" and "to firmly bind to" are translations of *katecho*). This is not a casual acceptance of the concept – but a binding to the life of the recipient. A second emphasis of the BINDING nature of the recipient (after #3 above) should help to clarify that it must be a serious and real choice to be effective.

Sixth, The Gospel was the highest priority message for the apostle to bring to the Corinthian people (the term *protos* is translated "of first importance" – 3a). He taught them much over the one and one half years he was with them – but nothing was of higher importance in the public ministry.

Seventh, Paul possessed the gospel before he shared it with them (the term "received" is again the term from verse one – *paralambano* – or "choose"). Though this isn't essential, it shows that it was intentional on his part. The gospel, because of its importance in HIS LIFE, was a burning message in the face of lost men and women.

Eighth, The message includes defined historical facts: the substitutional atoning literal death of Jesus for SIN (not politics), the fact of His physical burial in a tomb, and the literal understanding of the physical body's resurrection from the dead (15:5,6). A message without the components is a different message.

Ninth, The facts were prophesied from the Scriptures – the very Word of God (15:5). The narrative of Jesus' ministry was drawn from the prophets of old – and not some contrived story. In fact, without an understanding of the Hebrew Scriptures, one could not grasp the judicial terms of sin's separation, and a sacrifice's atoning nature.

Tenth, The facts of the case were verified by many in the early community, and in Paul's personal experience (15:8-11). Peter offered in *2 Peter 1:16 For we did not follow cleverly devised tales when we made known to you the power and coming of our Lord Jesus Christ, but we were eyewitnesses of His majesty.* Without predictive prophecy, the gospel is just a story made by men. Because God made promises, God keeps His promises, and the *Bible* contains His promises – we can see that Jesus fulfilled God's promises. No *Bible* – no salvation.

The message is spelled out in the Word, and is not fuzzy. People who preach the facts of the history with the call to surrender are offering the Gospel. People who don't – aren't. There is still one more myth I want to explore in the rest of the first chapter...

Myth 3: Political- Men put the whole thing together! The message of Jesus was a contrived political control.

Dan Brown asserted the Bible was put together by men for political control. Many a professor today will accept and teach a version of that notion – that the Church gave us the *Bible*, and the apostles contrived it. Others place the message later in the hands of Church Councils. What is the testimony of Paul?

Galatians 1:11 For I would have you know, brethren, that the gospel which was preached by me is not according to man. 12 For I neither received it from man, nor was I taught it, but [I received it] through a revelation of Jesus Christ. 13 For you have heard of my former manner of life in Judaism, how I used to persecute the church of God beyond measure and tried to destroy it; 14 and I was advancing in Judaism beyond many of my contemporaries among my countrymen, being more extremely zealous for my ancestral traditions. 15 But when God, who had set me apart [even] from my mother's womb and called me through His grace, was pleased 16 to reveal His Son in me so that I might preach Him among the Gentiles, I did not immediately consult with flesh and blood, 17 nor did I go up to Jerusalem to those who were apostles before me; but I went away to Arabia, and returned once more to Damascus. 18 Then three years later I went up to Jerusalem to become acquainted with Cephas, and stayed with him fifteen days. 19 But I did not see any other of the apostles except James, the Lord's brother. 20 (Now in what I am writing to you, I assure you before God that I am not lying.) 21 Then I went into the regions of Syria and Cilicia. 22 I was [still] unknown by sight to the churches of Judea which were in Christ; 23 but only, they kept hearing, "He who once persecuted us is now preaching the faith which he once tried to destroy." 24 And they were glorifying God because of me.

Paul said that he didn't GET the gospel from a man, nor COLLABORATE with another man or committee to put the message together. He got the message when Jesus gave it to him. People can accept that as truth, or they can reject it – but that was his claim. He said he sought to destroy the work in ignorance, and God grabbed his heart and showed His Son to Paul. Rather than send him to a school to learn of Jesus, God offered him a unique discipleship sitting in the desert at the feet of the risen Jesus. Three years passed, and Paul still didn't "check in" – he simply learned from Christ. When that time was over, Paul visited Peter and stayed in Jerusalem for fifteen days. He spoke to Peter and was encouraged by James, but the others didn't meet him. He kept a low profile until God called him out of a prayer meeting as a missionary to the Gentiles.

The myth that the gospel message was contrived by men is at the heart of the message of non-believers. **If the message didn't come from God, as they claim, then we offer nothing in the church by way of a true path of reconciliation to God, if there even is one.** Let me say it another way: If men made up the story of God sending His Son to Earth to die for the sins of man, then we are all lost. We have given ourselves to a well-crafted lie. The changes you have seen happen in your life aren't real. That healed marriage – that was just your imagination. That imprisoned criminal that is now out and serving God in his community – no, he is a fake. That moment when you heard God speak into your heart with the assurance of love and felt His touch as He pulled you to repentance – that was all a farce. You and I are just lost and hopeless. Good news is a myth. Nothing awaits us after this life but an end, period.

Let's be as clear as possible: **Either there is a god or there is not.** If there is NOT than we are observing a highly ordered universe that emerged without plan or purpose from chaos, organizing itself on the basis of random principles that gathered by happenstance to bring all things together. Stardust from an unknown source delved into an accidental "big bang" – with dust that eventually came together and made planets, lakes, fish, monkeys and man. The thousands of molecular systems of one human body just developed as genes sorted themselves out by no particular plan. You and I are a cosmic accident, a joke going nowhere. We live today, and die tomorrow, and none of it has any meaning whatsoever. Love, joy, art, progress – these words have little meaning beyond the pitiful one hundred years we walk on the planet. Those who went before are forever GONE and all we have are the memories and shreds of material work they left, until we ourselves fall to the earth. What does all that sound like? To me, it sounds like the depression of Solomon spilled out in Ecclesiastes.

He kept seeing no purpose, no meaning, no end, no justice, no light at the end of the tunnel. He said it many times in many ways – that life "under the sun" was vain, empty and useless. He was absolutely right...it is! If we seek truth "under the sun", inside the heliosphere of our solar system, life will not offer us sufficient truth to find meaning – because life's meaning is found in our Creator and His purpose for us! The good news is there is GOOD NEWS!

The Gospel is how God offers a restored relationship with man based solely on trust in the full payment for sin in Jesus Christ – a payment effective to reconcile the world to God and each other.

Dispelling Myths about the Gospel: Lessons in Galatians

Lesson Two: Galatians 2:1-21 "Myths Four and Five"

To anyone studying modern American trends, the story of the Massachusetts Bay Colony and the Puritan controversies will probably sound like a strange history of an entirely different people, but those struggling colonists are a vital part of our own history. They came to America largely FOR religious freedom, and their early struggles are some of the reasons people today abhor any crossover between state authority and church dogma. Let me illustrate that by retelling a story that used to be a part of our common American History curriculum, but has since been dropped. That is the story of an Antinomian Controversy of 1636-38.

The setting was the village of Boston of the seventeenth century. At the center of the controversy was a woman named Anne Hutchinson, a strong-minded Puritan daughter of an Anglican minister. Before she came from England, she embraced a Christian view that celebrated freedom in the gospel from what they called "the Moral Law" of the Hebrew Scriptures. Her Puritan minister was John Cotton who was forced to leave England, so Anne Hutchinson followed him to New England. She became influential among the settlement's women as she hosted them for a weekly *Bible* study in her home. She disagreed with the prevailing pastors of the colony that taught that in Christ one should embrace the lifestyle standards of the Hebrew law, and she criticized them openly, saying that they were preaching a "covenant of works" in denial of the "covenant of grace" she felt was true. So biting was her criticism, and so stirred were the women, that the colony's ministers held meetings in the autumn of 1636 hoping to regain unity. They began with a day of fasting and repentance on 19 January 1637. Sadly, they couldn't agree and the religious argument took on political ramifications. In the election of May 1637, these so-called "free grace" advocates were defeated in the gubernatorial race and magistrates who supported Anne Hutchinson and her friends were voted out of office. Her criticism didn't stop, and Anne Hutchinson was eventually held in detention in 1638 and excommunicated from the colony by a religious court. It seems hard to believe our pre-American colonial history tied the church so close to the state, but that is part of the historical pressure that Jefferson felt in the crafting of the Constitution.

Why did I start with a Puritan history lesson? Probably part of me is anticipating Thanksgiving coming soon, but that is not all. I recall that story to remind us of the issue we will examine today in our series on the "Myths of the Gospel" in Galatians 2. This lesson is about **antinomianism**. The "over-sized" term comes from two words: *anti*: "against" and *nomos*: Greek for "law". The theological concept means "one who holds to the belief that the message of the "gospel of grace" cancels any allegiance to the previous moral laws and precepts of lifestyle formerly taught under the Hebrew Law, because they believe that are both of "no use for salvation" and offer a contradiction to the message of "faith alone" for salvation.

Let us get off the big words and try to simplify the problem.

No sooner did the reformer Martin Luther explain that salvation was not earned, but a "gift of God" that came through simple faith in the completed work of Jesus on the Cross, a problem began in some groups that reacted to the "works" based churches they came out of into Protestantism. People grew up being told that they needed to keep the moral standards revealed in the Hebrew laws of the *Bible*, or they would go to Hell when they died. When Luther's preaching hit their ears, they realized that there was no work they could do to earn God's salvation, and they needed to trust the work that Jesus did dying in their place. They celebrated that as a gospel of grace, and began a walk with Jesus. In short order, some who did not want to live according to the standards of Scripture picked up on the message and began to sculpt a theology that taught, "Accept Jesus and live any way you want – because you are saved." They carefully divorced any lifestyle practice from the simple act of "receiving Jesus." Already at the time of Luther in the sixteenth century, they were dubbed by Luther and his followers in Germany as "antinomians" – "against any rules." By the time of Anne Hutchinson, that was old news… and they are with us to this day.

They make resurgence every time a movement wants to allow practices clearly not acceptable in the Scriptures. Today, they are all over the internet. Their message is simply this: You get salvation by believing that Jesus paid for your sin, not by surrendering anything. Surrender is a work, and Jesus doesn't save people by works. They get that idea, in my view, from misreading places in the Bible like Galatians 2, and they don't represent the true presentation of the gospel from the New Testament. Let's say carefully what the *Bible* truly teaches.

Key Principle: The gospel teaches that we don't earn a relationship with God through works (because it is a gift given to the undeserving) but we do offer God our lives and seek to obey Him in our walk now that we have been purchased by Him.

Let me unpack that.

First, we are saying that a right relationship with God comes only when we accept that the payment made by Jesus as He died on the cross as complete and full – nothing else needs to be accomplished to satisfy God for the mutiny of mankind in the Garden. The way became available by one and only one way – Jesus.

Second, we are saying that payment can only be applied to our lives when we ask Jesus to do so. That act is more than a decision to acknowledge what He did in history; it is an act of opening ourselves to His leading, and surrender to His mastery, as we believe what God says concerning the payment for sin in Jesus.

Third, the act of surrendering our mind and heart to God's Word concerning the Gospel continues as we take on a new life in Christ. That life is informed by the Scriptures, all of which are God-breathed and profitable for teaching, correction, and encouragement. In obedience to the Word, we earn no salvation – but in our saved state, we desire to live in obedience.

What does that mean?

It means that people who want to walk in disobedience need to really look deeply within to see if they truly want to confess Jesus as Lord or not. It means that believers DO live under a code of obedience that can be generally gauged by the Word of God. Let's look at the passage, and see if we can discern where the myths come from, and then we will answer them with a more accurate rendering of those same passages of Scripture. There are two myths we want to examine in addition to the three we saw in our last lesson…

Myth 4: Subversive - Paul's Gentile version of the gospel was different! Paul gave a different Gentile version of the message of Jesus that Jerusalem believers didn't agree to.

Some people acted as if Paul had a different message to Jews and to Gentiles concerning salvation – but he did not…

Galatians 2:1: Then after an interval of fourteen years, I went up again to Jerusalem with Barnabas, taking Titus along also. 2 It was because of a revelation that I went up; and I submitted to them the gospel which I preach among the Gentiles, but [I did so] in private to those who were of reputation, for fear that I might be running, or had run, in vain. 3 But not even Titus, who was with me, though he was a Greek, was compelled to be circumcised. 4 But [it was] because of the false brethren secretly brought in, who had sneaked in to spy out our liberty which we have in Christ Jesus, in order to bring us into bondage. 5 But we did not yield in subjection to them for even an hour, so that the truth of the gospel would remain with you. 6 But from those who were of high reputation (what they were makes no difference to me; God shows no partiality) – well, those who were of reputation contributed nothing to me. 7 But on the contrary, seeing that I had been entrusted with the gospel to the uncircumcised, just as Peter [had been] to the circumcised 8 (for He who effectually worked for Peter in [his] apostleship to the circumcised effectually worked for me also to the Gentiles), 9 and recognizing the grace that had been given to me, James and Cephas and John, who were reputed to be pillars, gave to me and Barnabas the right hand of fellowship, so that we [might] [go] to the Gentiles and they to the circumcised. 10 [They] only [asked] us to remember the poor– the very thing I also was eager to do.

There are a few initial observations we should mention before we get too far from our reading of the text:

First, Paul began in the middle of a defense that Gospel didn't come from man in verse one and we dealt with that in our previous lesson (2:1).

Second, Paul made clear that he was not offering a Gospel message to the pagan world that was not fully inspected by church leaders. He said in verse 2 that he "submitted to them the gospel which I preach" in the confines of a private chamber (2:2).

Third, the Apostles that reviewed the message agreed that Titus, because he was not a Jew, did not have the need to be circumcised in order to be saved (2:3). God's commands to the Jewish people informed the Gentiles of principles of what was important to God, but did not make them carry a law that was given as part of the unique covenant God held with the Jewish people.

Fourth, there were some who wanted all the church to be under the Law God gave specifically to the Jewish people (2:4-6). Paul affirmed that acquiescing to them would have corrupted the very core of the gospel itself.

Fifth, the apostles recognized that **God had a message to the uncircumcised that included the SAME PAYMENT FOR SIN in Christ (justification), but did not include the same lifestyle requirements (sanctification process) that God required of Jews** for "all their generations" in issues like Sabbath and circumcision (2:7-9). They recognized both groups existed and were one in Messiah's blood, but not the same in lifestyle. God told Jews to keep Sabbath for all their generations. He told them to circumcise their children as a unique sign forever. Gentiles didn't need to start doing those things, because they came under a different sanctification message. Everyone was saved the same way, but after salvation, bonded slaves lived differently than freedmen, men differently than women, Jews differently than Gentiles. Each would find sections of the New Testament defining specific calls for their group – though all were saved and "one in Christ."

Sixth, the Apostles DID require that Paul attach the new work of care for the poor through giving (2:10). This probably referred to the offerings taken up for the Jewish believers that were, at the time after Pentecost in Acts 2, still living in common in Jerusalem.

The point Paul was making was simply this: **I didn't tell Gentiles they needed to do the things God kept for the Jewish people**. I told them Jesus paid for their sin, and the sacrificial atonement system of the Jewish people would be of no use to them – along with all the other things Jews were told to do. I made clear to them they had a path of obedience to follow, but it wasn't the path of the Jewish people. At the same time, we need to be careful to underscore that Paul KEPT the Law and honored Jews to did so. He wasn't against keeping what God told them to keep for "all their generations". He wasn't embarrassed about honoring the Law. He was instructed by Jesus not to force Gentiles to keep that Law because it wasn't made for them.

Is there evidence for these statements? Yes, there is. I will offer it very briefly:

First, Acts 15 sets out the standards of the Jerusalem Council on Gentiles and their walk as a believing group. The group of apostles told the Gentiles in a letter from James that they would not make the Gentiles do the things Jews were already called to do. Jews wouldn't STOP doing them, but Gentiles didn't need to START doing them.

Second, Acts 21 made clear that **thousands of Jews kept on clinging to the practice of the Law after they came to Jesus** and the apostles honored them in front of Paul while Paul had no problem publicly affirming them in taking a vow to clear up any MISCONCEPTION that he was teaching Jews to STOP keeping the Laws God commanded them to do forever.

Third, in Acts 23:6 Paul claimed he continued to function as a Pharisee AFTER his mission journeys - making the overt claim to remaining Kosher and keeping Sabbath. If he didn't maintain the standards, he was flatly telling a lie to keep people happy. Does that sound like the Paul that was repeatedly beaten and stoned for NOT keeping people in authority happy?

Myth 5: Liberate: The gospel frees men from any requirement of obedience! Because we are saved by grace trough faith, we can live as we please and just believe in Jesus to get into Heaven.

There was a more important myth that developed – that of antinomianism – that Paul said Jesus wiped away all connection of believers in Jesus from the moral principles found in the Law.

Galatians 2:11 But when Cephas came to Antioch, I opposed him to his face, because he stood condemned. 12 For prior to the coming of certain men from James, he used to eat with the Gentiles; but when they came, he [began] to withdraw and hold himself aloof, fearing the party of the circumcision. 13 The rest of the Jews joined him in hypocrisy, with the result that even Barnabas was carried away by their hypocrisy. 14 But when I saw that they were not straightforward about the truth of the gospel, I said to Cephas in the presence of all, "If you, being a Jew, live like the Gentiles and not like the Jews, how [is it that] you compel the Gentiles to live like Jews? 15 "We [are] Jews by nature and not sinners from among the Gentiles; 16 nevertheless knowing that a man is not justified by the works of the Law but through faith in Christ Jesus, even we have believed in Christ Jesus, so that we may be justified by faith in Christ and not by the works of the Law; since by the works of the Law no flesh will be justified. 17 "But if, while seeking to be justified in Christ, we ourselves have also been found sinners, is Christ then a minister of sin? May it never be! 18 "For if I rebuild what I have [once] destroyed, I prove myself to be a transgressor. 19 "For through the Law I died to the Law, so that I might live to God. 20 "I have been crucified with Christ; and it is no longer I who live, but Christ lives in me; and the [life] which I now live in the flesh I live by faith in the Son of God, who loved me and gave Himself up for me. 21 "I do not nullify the grace of God, for if righteousness [comes] through the Law, then Christ died needlessly."

Again, before we address the myth, we must make some careful observations about the text:

First, Peter was making a mistake that required correction by Paul. The essence of the mistake was allowing Gentiles to be confused about their complete acceptance under the Gospel of Grace by their believing Jewish brothers. **Peter confused rabbinic standards with the Law**, and was embarrassed to eat in the presence of Gentile background Christians when being observed by Messianic Jews from Jerusalem that came for a visit. This wasn't the first time Peter made this particular mistake, as he verbalized an inaccurate statement in Acts 10 (2:11-13). There is no Hebrew Law that says a Jew cannot eat with a Gentile. There are laws about what can be served and how it is killed, but that wasn't the issue – it was the rabbinic standard of separation that was the mistake. It wasn't WHAT they ate in the text, it was that they ATE IT TOGETHER – and that was a rabbinic issue not a biblical one.

Second, full acceptance by God is at the heart of the Gospel message. Paul knew that ANY teaching that made those who were not required to keep the Law feel less than adequate before God required immediate and clear correction – because it would taint the Gospel message of salvation by full payment at the Cross (2:14a).

Third, Peter and Paul lived in the diaspora and were forced to make compromises in visiting Jerusalem for every feast, as Deuteronomy 16:16 commanded. They were **born Jews and struggled to maintain strict obedience in the days of the spread of the Roman Empire**. Frankly, without the rabbinic dispensations allowing an *anshai ma-amad* or "bystander" to take the place of a Jew at a feast, they would have been bound to Deuteronomy 16:16 and **had to be in Jerusalem in person three times a year**. Paul made clear it was nearly impossible for **THEM** to keep the Law, and they were **BORN INTO IT**. Paul could not believe Peter would force his Christian brothers into these same problems (2:14b-15a).

Fourth, Paul made clear that even the Jewish apostles that were raised with a love for the Law had long since concluded that the atonement law – **offering blood of bulls and goats to God in the temple to appease His wrath for a time – was no longer necessary**. (2:15b-16). Hebrews 9 made the same point. The old system was sacrifice, but it was incomplete because it never took care of ALL SIN. It needed to be repeated over and over. Jesus paid it all, once for all. The incomplete atonement of the Jerusalem Temple system was replaced by COMPLETE CLEANSING. No sacrifice (work of the Law for atonement) works – Now look at the end verses again:

Galatians 2:19: For through the Law I died to the Law, so that I might live to God. 20 "I have been crucified with Christ; and it is no longer I who live, but Christ lives in me; and the [life] which I now live in the flesh I live by faith in the Son of God, who loved me and gave Himself up for me. 21 I do not nullify the grace of God, for if righteousness [comes] through the Law, then Christ died needlessly.

Many people read those words and think, "There it is! **I am DEAD to the Law!** The Spirit will speak standards of living into my life and I **no longer need those old musty Hebrew Laws** anymore.

Is that what he said? No, and I can prove it...

First, the writer is Paul and we know from Acts that he didn't stop keeping feasts, taking vows and even going to the Temple. The whole story of his arrest in Acts 21 at the temple happened because he was AT THE TEMPLE TAKING A VOW – and that was after he traveled all three of his mission journeys.

Second, Paul and the other Apostles structured many of their arguments in the Epistles based on that Law in their writings to the churches. In one example, for instance, Paul wrote these words to the Corinthians: *"I am not speaking these things according to human judgment, am I? Or does not the Law also say these things?" (1 Cor. 9:8).* Why argue a point based on dead and ineffective old law?

Third, God used Paul later to record these words: *2 Timothy 3:16: All Scripture is inspired by God and profitable for teaching, for reproof, for correction, for training in righteousness, 17 so that the man of God may be adequate, equipped for every good work.*

Why didn't Paul make clear that **only New Testament writings were included** when most of what was called Scripture was the Hebrew Law and Writings?

What was Paul really saying?

Look at the end of the statement. Paul made clear what Law he was referring to – the kind that dealt with JUSTIFICATION. He said in *Galatians 2:21, I do not nullify the grace of God, for if righteousness [comes] through the Law, then Christ died needlessly.*

The issue was this: Did Gentiles need the Temple system with the atonement sacrifices that were symbolized in the dispersion by Sabbath keeping and circumcision – since people couldn't PHYSICALLY GO TO THE TEMPLE from all across the Roman world. When Jews spread far across the Mediterranean, the temple pilgrimage became a lifetime goal, not a three time a year experience. As such, the signs that you were under that system needed to be local and known.

Paul argued vehemently for the same truth that was revealed in Hebrews 9, that the Temple, the Priesthood, the atonement of animal blood –and all that went with it was no longer necessary because the full satisfaction for JUSTIFICATION was met at Calvary. On the cross of Messiah, Jesus died in my place – but in my salvation I ALSO DIED - to the command of Christ my Lord. I am now dead, and Christ's control dominates me. He lives in me. He rules me.

Look at those ending verses again, slowly and with a personal paraphrase to aid in our understanding:

Galatians 2:19: For according to the demands of the Atonement Law I was executed under my own sin according to the "blood for blood" requirement – so that I might live a new resurrected life full of God's empowering. I died with Christ on the Cross when I surrendered to Him. I am not my own, my life is now HIS. The life I continue to have in the flesh is one of believing what He says is true and trusting the payment He made in love for me. I do not cancel God's gift of Jesus by trusting in any animal's blood anymore, or Jesus could have avoided the Cross and left the old atonement law in place." (Randall D Smith paraphrase)

Now let's go back and consider the myth.

Can we honestly say these verses teach: The Gospel frees men from any requirement of obedience! Because we are saved by grace through faith, we can live as we please and just believe in Jesus to get into Heaven?

They say the OPPOSITE of that. They teach that coming to Christ is dying to self. It is letting Jesus take my life and steer it where He wants it to go.

Let's say it plainly:

Jesus is in charge of my wallet. I will make choices as to where I will work and how much, based on His command. I will choose to spend based on His leading. I will give back to Him according to His guidance.

Jesus is in charge of my entertainment. I will laugh at what He laughs at, because He is alive within me. I will sing what honors Him, because He hears every bar and note. I will watch what He would want me to watch, because He is sitting beside me as I look at my computer screen or into my flat screen TV.

Jesus is in charge of my sexuality. I will find my fulfillment where He says I should, so that I can lay my head on my pillow without shame or guilt. I will allow my heart to desire what He has said I may, and will carefully discipline my thoughts in areas He has forbidden, because He is alive in me and He is my King.

Jesus is in charge of my reputation. I will spend time serving people no one else cares about, and won't worry if people don't like their smell or their appearance – because I serve the Lord Christ. They are His children, and I am His servant!

Jesus is in charge of my schedule. If that means that He determines that my new assignment is 1000 hours in doctor's offices, I will go with the JOY that Jesus is represented wherever He sends me. I may not like the pain involved in the note I was sent to appear there, but I accept that my Savior knows where I need to be and when – because the moments of my life only have meaning because of Him.

Jesus is in charge of my goals. Whatever I can accomplish, whatever I can dream, whatever I can fulfill – I will pass every goal under His approving eye before I launch out as though I am my own – because I am HIS. He paid for my life. He paid for my accomplishments. All of them will be placed in front of Him at the end anyway – and only the ones He delights in will have any meaning!

There is no sense in which I am left to my own devices, but Jesus alive in me does not leave me in heaviness, but in JOY. I can BECOME Jesus in my office and in my community. I can show His love, and recall His promises to the hurting. I can also walk uprightly and according to His Word. I don't do it to EARN His love. I do it by His empowering and in His life flow – to His honor and His glory. Now, THAT is living!

The Gospel teaches that we don't earn a relationship with God through works (because it is a gift given to the undeserving) but we do offer God our lives and seek to obey Him in our walk now that we have been purchased by Him.

Dispelling Myths about the Gospel: Lessons in Galatians

Lesson Three: Galatians 3:1-29 "Myths Six and Seven"

The other day a box arrived at our front door. The days of anticipation were over as the long awaited replacement espresso machine was carefully exposed to the light of our dining room lamp. We were thrilled! The machine it replaced was a good one, but it died and we were left alone, espresso-less. In the beginning of our journey toward great coffee, my wife carefully researched online to find the best machine for us – because we take coffee seriously. She found what we both agreed was the perfect machine, but unfortunately, someone forgot to tell the assembly line to make it perfectly. After two years, we found ourselves with a kitchen counter "boat anchor" – a machine that wouldn't produce the coffee we bought it to make. Because we had it for a couple of years, we thought we were just going to have to bury it, move on past the period of mourning, and go buy another one. We are a tough lot, so we thought we could just bear it and move on. My sweetheart decided she would try to see if repairs could be made, and she called the company that made the machine. Answering the call was a thoughtful man who was obviously passionate about his morning espresso. She shared that our machine never seemed to work quite properly, and that it was now dead. He asked about the lot and registration number. "Were there parts?" my wife asked. The customer service representative's answer stunned her. "No, but I am sending you a label. Box the old unit and send it back to us. We are replacing the machine with a new one at no cost to you!" WOW! We were excited. Weeks passed... At long last, we were unboxing a new one, and it works very well! My point: some replacements are thrilling.

On the other hand, some replacements aren't a GOOD thing.

If you are a starting quarterback and you are moving the ball successfully down the field, you don't WANT to be replaced. If you are a middle child, a pet, or a spouse – you probably don't want to be replaced by someone or something else. It is a painful turn of events, and requires some justification – if any can even be made.

The strange thing is that so many *Bible* students and believers think God replaced His people. They think that His people, Israel, misbehaved and He replaced them with the church. Yet God expressed an undying love for that people. He spoke of her as a bride, and (because of what I believe is a mishandling of Scripture) they have concluded that God tossed out His wife when her behavior became so wrong, and she was replaced by Him. This isn't a new teaching, but it is a WRONG TEACHING. The Scripture says otherwise…

Key Principle: God the Father has a permanent irrevocable call to Israel that is entirely separate from the call of the Savior to His church.

Think about that principle, and don't drop away at this point. What has God's choice of Israel to do with YOU? Perhaps you are encountering God's Word today and you have a physical problem that your doctor cannot easily diagnose and resolve. Perhaps this month seems much bigger than the pile of money you have to cover the needs of it. Maybe you are worried about a child or grandchild, and you aren't sure they are making good decisions. Perhaps you are struggling with God about a blow you have had to your life recently. **How is learning about myths and misunderstandings from Galatians 3 going to help you with anything YOU REALLY CARE ABOUT?**

The answer is both simple and direct: God's call and God's promises are what you stand in, and what you need to be able to unreservedly trust in order to walk in confidence this week. If God is true to His Word, and His Word is not some kind of shell game or Ponzi scheme – you will be able to rest and face your problems with the confidence of His words: *I will never leave you nor forsake you.* However, if His Word is steeped in some unrecognizable code, and that simple promise we just stated is a cryptic reference to "I will never leave someone who may or may not be you but may forsake you if you don't behave," then let the worry begin.

In the simplest terms, God keeps His Word to the One to whom He gives it. He isn't fickle, and He isn't trying to be unduly complicated. That doesn't mean the *Bible* is full of monosyllabic words, but it does mean He isn't intentionally misleading people. The story of sin and redemption is complex, I will admit. At the same time, **the promises of God are clear, trustworthy and straightforward.** The twisting of God's Word has largely been due to either the misunderstanding of the poorly taught, or the torqueing of the text by those who have an agenda, and find an ally in the enemy of God's people – the Deceiver. Let's look at the myths, and remember they are much more relevant than they first appear. To begin, let's look at a popularly believed myth rooted in a misreading of Galatians 3:1-14…

Myth 6: There are New Jews - the Gospel permanently cancelled the Jewish marriage contract and replaced them! By faith, the Law was rendered meaningless and the Spirit made believers in Jesus into the new Jews, the new chosen people.

Where would one get such an idea? Many reformers of yesteryear thought it was, at least in part, the point of these words…

Galatians 3:1 You foolish Galatians, who has bewitched you, before whose eyes Jesus Christ was publicly portrayed [as] crucified? 2 This is the only thing I want to find out from you: did you receive the Spirit by the works of the Law, or by hearing with faith? 3 Are you so foolish? Having begun by the Spirit, are you now being perfected by the flesh? 4 Did you suffer so many things in vain– if indeed it was in vain? 5 So then, does He who provides you with the Spirit and works miracles among you, do it by the works of the Law, or by hearing with faith? 6 Even so Abraham BELIEVED GOD, AND IT WAS RECKONED TO HIM AS RIGHTEOUSNESS. 7 Therefore, be sure that it is those who are of faith who are sons of Abraham. 8 The Scripture, foreseeing that God would justify the Gentiles by faith, preached the gospel beforehand to Abraham, [saying], "ALL THE NATIONS WILL BE BLESSED IN YOU." 9 So then, those who are of faith are blessed with Abraham, the believer. 10 For as many as are of the works of the Law are under a curse; for it is written, "CURSED IS EVERYONE WHO DOES NOT ABIDE BY ALL THINGS WRITTEN IN THE BOOK OF THE LAW, TO PERFORM THEM." 11 Now that no one is justified by the Law before God is evident; for, "THE RIGHTEOUS MAN SHALL LIVE BY FAITH." 12 However, the Law is not of faith; on the contrary, "HE WHO PRACTICES THEM SHALL LIVE BY THEM." 13 Christ redeemed us from the curse of the Law, having become a curse for us– for it is written, "CURSED IS EVERYONE WHO HANGS ON A TREE"—14 in order that in Christ Jesus the blessing of Abraham might come to the Gentiles, so that we would receive the promise of the Spirit through faith.

Look closely at the text and what it says...It begins with some questions.

The first is **"Who tricked you?"** (3:1) You heard of the Crucifixion when we preached it to you, and now you seem to have need of something else. Who convinced you of that need?

A second question followed. **"When did you receive the empowering work of the Spirit of God?"** (3:2-3) If the Spirit moved at the time of coming to Christ, than why would they seek another form of justification, or go backwards into the now cancelled atonement system? (Remember the context of the verses is set in verse one in relationship to salvation through the crucifixion.) If a relationship with God is found at Calvary, than the atonement system is a step backward.

A third question was posed: **"Was all the suffering to stand apart in the teaching of salvation through Jesus alone a waste?"** (3:4)

A fourth question followed: **"Did God require you to keep or even know about the works involved in the atonement system for you to have both His Spirit and His miracles?"** (3:5)

From the four questions emerges an underlying principle that Paul wanted to make plain: **God used simple trust in His revealed Word as the standard of justification long before there ever was a set of revealed atonement laws** (3:6). – but the content of that truth has been expanded carefully over the ages.

Because the issue has always been trust in what God revealed to a particular generation that they must believe, you **Gentile believers are spiritually "children of Abraham" by means of your surrender to God's promises** apart from any system God gave to anyone else. (3:7)

Despite claims of Judaizers, **there were promises found in Genesis that show that God is not acting outside of His Word saving people outside the atonement laws given to the Jewish people** (3:8).

Gentile believers today, Paul said, **are offered justification** (a relationship with God whereby He is utterly satisfied by the payment for sin) **just like Abraham was** – because of surrender to God's Word to them (3:9). Abraham didn't need any atonement system beyond trusting what God said, and neither do Gentile believers who are reading this epistle to Galatia.

Joining the atonement law system of the temple, where there is always a continued need for more sacrifices and more observances for justification, is **stepping backward into the curse of continuity that has been fully satisfied** (3:10). In the temple atonement system, the minute you stop doing it, God's satisfaction is left unsatisfied, and the penalty of sin is left upon you.

The simple fact is that the **atonement system has been replaced, because it did not have the ability to justify** – it simply atoned (and even that was temporary). (3:11).

At the heart of the atonement law is a series of **continuous performances** – practices of the law. They were fine to cover sin in atonement, but there are many who mistook the practice for what energized God's satisfaction. That is, and has always been, faith – the belief in what God said. Perfectly good bulls and goats, carefully sacrificed, were of **NO EFFECT on God's satisfaction over man's sinful mutiny in the Garden if the spilling of their blood was not done by someone who truly accepted God's Word**, and practiced in faith. (3:12).

> **Jesus' work fully purchased us,** removing us from the temporary atonement system by becoming the sin-laden sacrifice – and in that He removed the "curse" of needing constant new installments to satisfy God throughout our life (3:13).

> **Jesus paid for sin as a substitute** in order that God may fulfill His promise to offer a direct blessing to the world by faith that did not require coming under the atonement temple system of the Jewish people (3:14).

Perhaps the best way to illustrate the point that Paul was making to the Galatians is to look at a candle or an oil lamp.

For centuries, if you wanted to light your home, you used an oil lamp or a candle. They work well – so well that we measure light output in candlepower. Yet, they had a troublesome shortcoming. They didn't work well in drafty rooms or outside in the wind. A windscreen lantern was developed, but that cut down significantly the amount of light one obtained from the candle or lamp. More recently, inventors offered us the more reliable alternative of the flashlight. It works indoors and out, and it doesn't flicker in the wind. It is a BETTER LIGHT. That is not to say that lamps and candles are BAD – they aren't. It does mean they were temperamental in a way that flashlights are.

I know the analogy has a breakdown because flashlights have bulbs that break and batteries that fail – but I think you get the point. The atonement law was fine to save someone, but it was part of a system that required constant maintenance. That had the benefit of allowing people to feel deeply connected to the constant maintenance of their soul, but it also meant that many things could go wrong in their ability to truly maintain their standing before a satisfied God. Jesus came to end all of that uncertainty, and offer a single sacrifice permanent solution. **He didn't replace His people; He replaced the atonement system they trusted in to satisfy God.**

The point of Galatians IS NOT that the Law of God was bad, but that the atonement laws of God were deficient in the sense of permanency which God built into the system. He would later open a direct door to the whole world for a time, so that people could be saved without direct connection to the Jewish people at all. A villager along the Coco River between Honduras and Nicaragua need not know a Jew or even truly understand much of the sacrificial system in order to come into a relationship with God in which God is fully satisfied. They need only know Jesus.

Lest we misapply Paul's statements about the atonement law's deficiency, and we inadvertently take a swipe at the whole of the Torah, remember that God GAVE the Law of Moses, and Jews loved that Law even AFTER JESUS CAME (Acts 21). The perfection and holiness of the Law is oft celebrated in the Scriptures. The part of that law that was wholly replaced was atonement law, how a mutinous rebel comes into communion with God and satisfies the debt of sin before Him. Jews were given a temporary system that THEY NEEDED for a time. While Moses was getting Levitical Law and plans for a tabernacle, the people were at the bottom of Mt. Sinai making a calf and devising their own system of sacrifice – because they NEEDED ONE. It worked for as long, and well as candles lit homes, and it was replaced by something better.

Keep a keen eye on the context of Paul's argument. He isn't addressing whether Jews should keep a Sabbath or circumcise their children – he is arguing whether the symbols of the atonement laws were helpful or harmful in a Gentile context. The Sabbath, circumcision, and feasts of the Lord were the only ties that Jews in the Roman world outside of their homeland had to hold them together – and Gentiles joining in those symbols would find themselves entering an atonement system that placed them back under the temple system of authority, and the sacrificial system of satisfying God. It negated one reason for the work of Jesus. It shut off the direct door between the Gentile world and God – and truncated salvation back through the Jewish people – which wasn't what God wanted for this age.

Misunderstanding the limited argument Paul was making is what caused the next myth to flow.

Myth 7: Fulfilled - The Law has accomplished its mission! The Law of Moses was just a tutor that brought the world to the Savior, but is now retired – so we can live life without the constraints of the Hebrew Law.

Galatians 3:15 Brethren, I speak in terms of human relations: even though it is [only] a man's covenant, yet when it has been ratified, no one sets it aside or adds conditions to it. 16 Now the promises were spoken to Abraham and to his seed. He does not say, "And to seeds," as [referring] to many, but [rather] to one, "And to your seed," that is, Christ. 17 What I am saying is this: the Law, which came four hundred and thirty years later, does not invalidate a covenant previously ratified by God, so as to nullify the promise. 18 For if the inheritance is based on law, it is no longer based on a promise; but God has granted it to Abraham by means of a promise. 19 Why the Law then? It was added because of transgressions, having been ordained through angels by the agency of a mediator, until the seed would come to whom the promise had been made. 20 Now a mediator is not for one [party only]; whereas God is [only] one. 21 Is the Law then contrary to the promises of God? May it never be! For if a law had been given which was able to impart life, then righteousness would indeed have been based on law. 22 But the Scripture has shut up everyone under sin, so that the promise by faith in Jesus Christ might be given to those who believe. 23 But before faith came, we were kept in custody under the law, being shut up to the faith which was later to be revealed. 24 Therefore the Law has become our tutor [to lead us] to Christ, so that we may be justified by faith. 25 But now that faith has come, we are no longer under a tutor. 26 For you are all sons of God through faith in Christ Jesus. 27 For all of you who were baptized into Christ have clothed yourselves with Christ. 28 There is neither Jew nor Greek, there is neither slave nor free man, there is neither male nor female; for you are all one in Christ Jesus. 29 And if you belong to Christ, then you are Abraham's descendants, heirs according to promise.

If what Paul was addressing in the TUTOR of Galatians was what we now call the "Old Testament," then can we toss it out of our *Bible* because it doesn't mean anything now? I hear this all the time. "Capital punishment"? Don't worry, Jesus threw out the Law. The tutor is dead." "Sexual standards? If it isn't repeated in the New Testament, it isn't really something we need to worry about." Really? I would argue that Paul said those observations are 100% true of atonement law, but totally and utterly UNTRUE of the lifestyle principles derived from the rest of the Torah Law. If the tutor is the Old Testament, the sexual practice of bestiality is IN (because it is only specifically addressed in the OT) and 2 Timothy 3:16 is OUT (because those Scriptures from the Old Testament are ALL retired with the tutoring that led us to Christ). The argument is: Jesus came, so all the laws that let us know we are sinners are now only important if repeated in the New Testament. That will leave us with a Christian message that doesn't take MOST of what God said seriously because of their misunderstanding of the argument of Galatians 3.

What DID Paul say in the passage?

- God's words were exacting in His promise about atonement law – **He promised ONE would come to open a direct door for the world** to Him through a specific Jew – in place of the door only available for centuries through the atonement system of a Temple operated by and for Jewish people (3:15-16).
- The promise was made before the atonement system was set in place, and that promise was not negated by the institution of the sacrificial system that came after it (3:17-18).
- Why create an atonement system that wouldn't last forever? (3:19-20) **God's promise lived beneath the whole sacrificial system to prepare us for the One who came to be our sacrifice**. It dealt with sin at the time, and set up the substitutional atonement system so we understood the meaning of the death of Messiah when it happened.
- If atonement law was complete, no other way would have been opened (3:21). The message of the promise of satisfaction by trusting the payment of Jesus opened the direct door for all men without the need for the Temple atonement system (3:22).
- Under atonement law, men were in the custody of that law, waiting for a provision that would open direct access to God

from anywhere in the world apart from atonement law (3:23-24).

- **The direct door of full satisfaction of sin by complete trust in the payment by Jesus' blood has swung the door wide open to a relationship with the Living God for all who trust this message** (3:25-27). All come in the same way, no distinction as to how we get to God – rather all clinging to the same promises and using the same door – the door long ago promised (3:28).
- Spiritually, **we who know God through Jesus are "faith descendants" and "promise inheritors"** – a position to be celebrated (3:29).
-

Does that mean Paul thought God was done with the Jewish people? Was this a REPLACEMENT POLICY of the Jewish people?

Does that mean Paul believed that followers of Jesus became the NEW SONS OF ABRAHAM displacing the old sons of Abraham? Not at all. Paul said just the opposite in his argument in Romans 10 and 11:

The context was Israel's rejection of the gospel and their need to understand the justification message of the church. He wrote:

Romans 10:1 Brethren, my heart's desire and my prayer to God for them is for [their] salvation. 2 For I testify about them that they have a zeal for God, but not in accordance with knowledge. 3 For not knowing about God's righteousness and seeking to establish their own, they did not subject themselves to the righteousness of God. 4 For Christ is the end of the law for righteousness to everyone who believes.

Clearly, Paul said that a right relationship before God in salvation (justification) comes ONLY through the sacrifice of Jesus – no animal atonement works because that system was

OVER. Jews were clinging to sacrifices of atonement and denying cleansing in Christ. That snubbed God's gift and continued the rebellion against following God's Word as it became available to them in their day. He went on to point out how offensive the gospel was, because the direct door of salvation bypassed the system that Jewish authorities continued to control...

Romans 10:12: For there is no distinction between Jew and Greek; for the same [Lord] is Lord of all, abounding in riches for all who call on Him; 13 for "WHOEVER WILL CALL ON THE NAME OF THE LORD WILL BE SAVED."

Many Jews saw this as a negative that God took them from the center stage, but the opposite was true – the Gospel is GOOD NEWS. Far more could have a relationship with God than ever before around the globe. Still it stung... because God now had a direct relationship with the world apart from them, and it made them mad...

Romans 10:19 But I say, surely Israel did not know, did they? First Moses says, "I WILL MAKE YOU JEALOUS BY THAT WHICH IS NOT A NATION, BY A NATION WITHOUT UNDERSTANDING WILL I ANGER YOU." 20 And Isaiah is very bold and says, "I WAS FOUND BY THOSE WHO DID NOT SEEK ME, I BECAME MANIFEST TO THOSE WHO DID NOT ASK FOR ME."

At that point, Paul addressed Israel's future with God. He started with a question in Romans 11:1.

Romans 11:1 I say then, God has not rejected His people, has He? May it never be! For I too am an Israelite, a descendant of Abraham, of the tribe of Benjamin.

He made clear that a remnant of Jews already recognized that justification (full cleansing in Jesus) replaced atonement (temporary covering of animal sacrifice). He made clear that God had long before promised a time when Israel's eyes would be dark for a time:

Romans 11:8 ...just as it is written, "GOD GAVE THEM A SPIRIT OF STUPOR, EYES TO SEE NOT AND EARS TO HEAR NOT, DOWN TO THIS VERY DAY."

Paul renewed a sense of hope for his fellow Messianic believers about their brothers and sisters in the flesh who did not yet believe in Messiah's sacrifice, but kept pushing ahead with the atonement system. He wrote:

Romans 11:11 I say then, they did not stumble so as to fall, did they? May it never be! But by their transgression salvation [has come] to the Gentiles, to make them jealous. 12 Now if their transgression is riches for the world and their failure is riches for the Gentiles, how much more will their fulfillment be!

He clarified the coming salvation of the Jewish people as a people a few verses later. He wrote:

Romans 11:25 For I do not want you, brethren, to be uninformed of this mystery – so that you will not be wise in your own estimation – that a partial hardening has happened to Israel until the fullness of the Gentiles has come in; 26 and thus all Israel will be saved; just as it is written, "THE DELIVERER WILL COME FROM ZION; HE WILL REMOVE UNGODLINESS FROM JACOB." 27 "THIS IS MY COVENANT WITH THEM, WHEN I TAKE AWAY THEIR SINS." 28 From the standpoint of the gospel they are enemies for your sake, but from the standpoint of [God's] choice, they are beloved for the sake of the fathers; 29 for the gifts and the calling of God are irrevocable. ...
and then Paul breaks into praise for God's marvelous plan!

Let's close up this lesson where we opened it:

- He replaced the temporary atonement system with permanent cleansing and removed Israel from the center role she played until her time comes back.

- God means what He says. When He called Israel His beloved, the apple of His eye, His everlasting love – He wasn't speaking metaphorically. He spoke of the promises as coming "from the loins of the Patriarchs" – not some spiritual hocus pocus about someone else. God promised Abraham that He would bless the world with a direct line to Him that was available after Adam and before Moses – but was truncated through Israel after Moses. God was going to open the door through One Israelite, for a period of time, before he made all Israel return to Him.

- He has a future for Israel - the literal, physical children of Abraham through Isaac and Jacob are still children of promise. God isn't done with them yet. Paul knew it and made it clear in Romans 10 and 11.

Why should you care?

Because the God you trust for salvation and eternity is exacting in His desires, specific in His communication and ever faithful in His delivery. He isn't fuzzy on truth. God knows when He is satisfied with a payment for sin. **God isn't interested in our devising a different system to be acceptable to Him other than the one He laid out in His Word.**

The God that is still at work over generations and thousands of years to specifically fulfill every detail of His promises is also preparing the place you are heading if you know Jesus. Look up! Home is under construction and the Builder won't leave a single knob off the cabinets. **God the Father has a permanent irrevocable call to Israel that is entirely separate from the call of the Savior to His church… and that is good for all of us. It reminds us of the faithfulness God pledges to His every promise.**

Dispelling Myths about the Gospel:
Lessons in Galatians

Lesson Four: Galatians 4:1-31
"Myths Eight and Nine"

Tis the season to be jolly! I love the sound of that! Holiday...doesn't that simple WORD make you feel good? The word is a contraction of two old English terms – "holy" and "day." It was a term to denote a special remembrance or celebration, originally related to religious things – hence the term "holy." It is a time filled with excitement, a kitchen oven warming the cool of the morning and the smell of delights that no one can resist! What a JOYOUS time of year.

Holidays are at the heart of our identity. They are what communicate our connections that we feel strongly about.

- We stop our normal life to go to a **wedding** because we have a connection to the people who are joining themselves together.
- As Americans, we have a picnic on **Independence Day** because we want to show that we value the *Declaration of Independence* written by men long ago, and identify with the country God used them to create.
- We eat cake at a **birthday** party to signal a special connection to the one that has made it to the milestone of another year on the planet!
- We have our turkey at **Thanksgiving** to recall the miraculous survival of a small band of Christian pilgrims to the shores of what later became the Massachusetts Bay Colony.
- We gather in our churches and in our homes at **Christmas** to recall a day, long ago, when God broke into human history. That One replaced the sacrifices of bulls and goats made by one small group of people in Judea with a perfect one-time sacrifice through Messiah that offered a direct connection through faith in God's

promise – apart from the temple calendar and the animal sacrifices.

Holidays show allegiance. They symbolize commitment to something or someone. They announce connection to events and people both in the past and in our lives that have significance to us.

We have only sketchy views of such holidays that were celebrated by ancient human beings– and most of that comes from the Bronze Age. Most any scholar, whether secular or Christian, will likely tell you that the most complete information available on ancient holidays is from the *Bible*. The "Feasts of the Lord" represent the most clearly explained early documentation concerning festivals and feast days. The Chinese, Hittites, Indus River civilization, and Egyptians certainly had many festivals, but we have much less detail on most of them than what is included in the *Bible* from the Late Bronze period (that *Bible* students know as the time of the Exodus and Conquest of Canaan). Long ago, in the wilderness desolation of the Sinai Peninsula, the *Bible* records that God took an extended family that had been oppressed in Egypt and turned them into a nation. He gave them a central worship place, a set of unique God-given Laws, and a series of memorial holidays. Leviticus 23 and passages like it called the Jewish people to these "Feasts of the Lord." Those holidays were a connection marker to God that included a weekly Sabbath – something God called Jews uniquely from among men to keep for "all their generations" (Ex. 31:31). When direct access to God opened, many Jews wanted Gentile-born believers to simply "act like Jews" because that was what made sense to them. Today in the church, many wrongly teach that Jews need to simply "act like Gentiles" to join the church. Neither is a proper reflection of the text of the New Testament if viewed up close.

Key Principle: God kept in place unique markers for the Jewish people (because He has a future plan for

them) that the church around the world need not be concerned about adopting, no matter what pressure they receive to do so.

As we have been studying in Galatians, a NEW COVENANT system was being set in place that not only encompassed the Jewish people, but prior to their national embrace (that hasn't happened yet) it gave direct access for salvation to anyone on Earth apart from Israel – if they would only believe what God communicated about justification. Every man, every woman, as well as every child old enough to discern truth – are called to simply trust that what Jesus did at the Cross of Calvary was sufficient for their salvation, whether of Jewish or Gentile background. One day that same New Covenant forged in the blood of Messiah will lead even the most stubborn hearts of Israel back into the arms of God the Father, Who now patiently awaits the humbling of His estranged wife, the nation of Israel.

Yet, during this time of direct access to God through Christ, **God kept in place the unique markers for Israel they were commanded to obey:**

- Hebrews 4 reminds the Jewish believer that there was still a Sabbath *"on the day that God rested..."* It was not replaced with Sunday, for that was not the same day of the week, nor is there any command to do so in Scripture. At the same time, Colossians 2 sternly warned the Gentile church not to allow Jewish people to tell them what day to meet – for that command was not given to them but to Jews who would follow God.

- The circumcision commanded to Abraham for *"all his future generations"* in Genesis 17:12 continued to be a marker for that unique people, even with the coming of Jesus. To make that clear, Paul circumcised his disciple Timothy (Acts 16:3) because his mother was Jewish but his father was Greek, and therefore he had not been circumcised. Yet his other disciple, Titus, was not circumcised as a man born of two Gentile parents.

- Certain celebrations were commanded to be a part of Jewish life "for all their generations." One such command regarded Passover and Unleavened Bread (Ex. 12:14 and 12:17). Another, the "Day of Atonement" or "Yom Kippor" was also specified to be continued "throughout their generations" (Lev. 23:41). Paul kept the feasts as best he was able. Acts 20 relates that Paul was counting on making the Feast of Shavuot (Pentecost) in Jerusalem (20:16) and was counting the Sabbaths (20:6-7) to make the journey, according to the Jewish reckoning of time – because he was a Jew. In Acts 21, he went to the Temple to take a public vow AFTER his three mission journeys in the name of Jesus.

Paul **understood the difference between God's Jewish program and His direct access program in Messiah** and wanted that **clear** in his ministry, to be an offense to no one in areas of obedience given to the Jewish people for all their generations, **while not allowing Jews to bind over the symbols and the now defunct atonement system of the Temple to the new Gentile church**. Those symbols would confuse the Gentiles, and place them under the control of the Sanhedrin – many who did not know Jesus and did not acknowledge (or perhaps even know) that a replacement of the atonement system had already been completed.

Churches that do not distinguish between how Jews and Gentiles are called to live AFTER they are saved by the blood of Jesus invite error, just as those who replace the unique people of the sons of Abraham with the spiritual sons of promise in the Gentile church. **Both Jew and Gentile are one in Messiah, but not one in lifestyle – for God told one group to do things forever that He never told the other to start**. That is what caused confusion in the first century, and what gave rise to most of Paul's epistles. It was the largest problem he faced, and we are still facing it today – only with the church now holding the upper hand and Jews being relegated to replacement of lifestyle.

That mistake has led to two other myths that many believers follow that are worth exploring, as Paul offered insight in Galatians…

Myth 8: New Calendar! The Gospel cancelled the feasts of the Lord and freed all believers from the Hebrew festival calendar.

There are **three groups of people in church circles** that I run into today **in regards to the feasts and the calendar:**

One group simply says it was abandoned , a relic of another time, not to be used as anything but a teaching device from history. They really don't offer a great answer to the "for all your generations" issue – but say Jesus replaced that without any grammar support for their position. That is what I was taught growing up in the faith, and I find it to bypass a literal view of Scripture. If that view is right, forever might mean temporary – and that troubles me. "All your generations" might mean, "'til Jesus comes" – and I cannot reconcile that problem.

A second group insists that since God set them up, they must be for everyone today. They point to the church's position as one of compromise and error, if we don't build sukkahs (temporary shelters associated with the Feast of Tabernacles) and light candles for Sabbath on Friday night. These believers try to get their church to look more like a synagogue and do things that are associated with the Jewish people. Yet, when I examine the Scriptures carefully, I wonder why we would need the New Testament at all. Why didn't Paul simply write to every congregation, "Come to Jesus, then keep the Law!" The complicated formula of two ways of following one single Savior seems to speak against that view. This group doesn't have a cogent view of what a Judaizer is – and that troubles me as well.

A third group, well known to many who study the *Bible* south of the Mason-Dixon Line in the cultural Christianity of the *Bible*-belt **are those who believe we "spiritually keep Sabbath", except the day got moved and the restrictions got dropped.** This group represents most of the believers you will meet in town who say "My Sabbath is Sunday!" Yet, they cannot point to any command that moved the day, nor can they show that they restrict themselves on Sunday in a way that marked true Sabbath observance. They routinely do forbidden things for a Sabbath on a day other than the one specified and claim they are "keeping their Sabbath." I am absolutely confident that Paul would not identify with that in any way.

What is God calling a believer to do regarding Sabbath and festivals?

Galatians 4:1: Now I say, as long as the heir is a child, he does not differ at all from a slave although he is owner of everything, 2 but he is under guardians and managers until the date set by the father. 3 So also we, while we were children, were held in bondage under the elemental things of the world. 4 But when the fullness of the time came, God sent forth His Son, born of a woman, born under the Law, 5 so that He might redeem those who were under the Law, that we might receive the adoption as sons. 6 Because you are sons, God has sent forth the Spirit of His Son into our hearts, crying, "Abba! Father!" 7 Therefore you are no longer a slave, but a son; and if a son, then an heir through God. 8 However at that time, when you did not know God, you were slaves to those which by nature are no gods. 9 But now that you have come to know God, or rather to be known by God, how is it that you turn back again to the weak and worthless elemental things, to which you desire to be enslaved all over again? 10 You observe days and months and seasons and years. 11 I fear for you, that perhaps I have labored over you in vain. 12 I beg of you, brethren, become as I [am], for I also [have become] as you [are]. You have done me no wrong; 13 but you know that it was because of a bodily illness that I preached the gospel to you the first time; 14 and that which was a trial to you in my bodily condition you did not despise or loathe, but you received me as an angel of God, as Christ Jesus [Himself]. 15 Where then is that sense of blessing you had? For I bear you witness that, if possible, you would have plucked out your eyes and given them to me. 16 So have I become your enemy by telling you the truth? 17 They eagerly seek you, not commendably, but they wish to shut you out so that you will seek them. 18 But it is good always to be eagerly sought in a commendable manner, and not only when I am present with you. 19 My children, with whom I am again in labor until Christ is formed in you—20 but I could wish to be present with you now and to change my tone, for I am perplexed about you.

Paul's basic argument is that God gave to the Jewish people pictures that forecast the future. He left them under a temporary system of atonement (sacrifice) to teach them about sin and the blood required to satisfy Him in light of the mutiny.

- A Picture (4:1-2) In the Roman system, certain domestic slaves were given the work of watching over children. In the case of male children, and in particular the master's sons, a *paidagogos* (sometimes translated a "tutor") was placed in a position of responsibility over the child's behavior, instruction and development (both physical and social). That tutor exercised control over the child when necessary, in spite of the fact that the child would later (upon reaching the arranged age set by the *Paterfamilias* "father" of the household) be his master. Atonement was our slave-master until the time of its replacement.

- A Point (4:3) Mankind was set under a temporary guardian in the atonement law, bound to the blood and livestock sacrifice – an earthy, gritty, bloody arrangement.

- A Promise (4:4-8) At the appropriate moment God sent Jesus through a young Jewish mother who kept that atonement law (and paid careful attention to the raising of a lamb all her days in her home). That child grew to be the Lamb of sacrifice, and in His sacrifice, the door opened for direct connection to God through His death, even for those who were formerly under the atonement sacrifice for salvation, the Jewish people. Those who believe are "adopted" into the place of sons, though they weren't born naturally to that place. As sons, we can cry out directly to our Father, and He hears us! Because the direct door is open and we can (by belief in the sacrifice of Jesus) be full sons apart from the atonement system, the new adopted sons have been named as full heirs – a far cry from their former estate as simple slaves of another master.

- A Problem (4:9-11) How can those from the old atonement system now entice you to go back to keeping track of sacrifices and joining a fully replaced system? If you go back to the sacrificial calendar and all the feasts and offerings, you plunge backward into a system that was never given to you, and cannot help you. I fear all the ministry to you will be wasted when you turn your back on God's full acceptance by grace through faith in Jesus, and His blood sacrifice alone!

Paul made clear there were Jews that arrived in Galatia and implored them to abandon the "by the blood of Jesus, once for all" plan of salvation and go backward into the atonement system of sacrifice and the control of the Temple in Jerusalem. These Galatians, Gentile born, spirit-filled believers were being pulled back to a system that no longer held the key to a relationship with God, by a people who wanted to control their lives. Paul pleaded with them:

- A Plea (4:12-20) Paul essentially said, "I am begging you to become like me (one who does not trust the old atonement system for justification at all). You received me so well, in spite of the fact that I was sick when I was with you in the beginning (you know how I struggled). Where is that reception now? You know I would have given you anything then, so how is it now you struggle to trust me? (4:17-20) Let me be straight with you – the men from Judea are working hard to block you from hearing me because they want you to seek them alone. I am deeply concerned about you, that your trust in Christ will be diverted."

Some are thrown off by the phrase, "become as I am," because there is abundant evidence in the book of Acts that he kept the feasts and vows all the way through his career. The issue wasn't whether or not Jews kept the Sabbath, circumcision, and calendar given to them "for all their generations," it was whether the plan God had for that obedience had anything to do with the justification formula.

When people read this, they are quick to want to DO the things Paul did – but that isn't what he was saying. It was never wrong for Jews to keep observing their feasts or vows as a Jewish believer. **What WAS wrong was to mistake those things as having any bearing on the formula for justification – Jesus alone saves.** He saves Jews – for the Gospel "is the power of God to save, to the Jew first...". He saves Gentiles – "then also to the Greek" – all the same way (see Romans 1:16-17). Besides that, no one was to appropriate Jewish sanctification standards into the life of a Gentle – they weren't given to Gentiles . The only Gentiles ,that were told to keep them were the ones living AMONG THE JEWISH PEOPLE, and that wasn't the case in any Galatian church.

Remember, though obedience to the "forever" commands like Sabbath, circumcision, and the Feasts of the Lord were not dismissed from the Jewish believer, they weren't to be observed for salvation – but rather for showing a unique Jewish identity. Interestingly, that system will show up again in the Millennial Rule of Christ – where Jesus demonstrates how He intended it all to show a perfect picture of His work.

What Paul said was essentially this in 4:1-20: God set up an atonement tutor that has been set aside now that we have reached the time God set to open direct access to men everywhere to Himself without the Jewish people and their leaders. **Come to know God through Jesus**, and you will have a direct, complete and full relationship with a loving Father. **Don't try to tie yourself to the defunct atonement system –** that is finished, replaced, and utterly unnecessary!

Myth 9: The Law enslaves! Heaven broke the curse of the Law and set us free from all its restrictions.

Again, we see how easily this myth could grab hold of people. Jews were pressing them to act like Jews, and Paul was pressing them to be distinct as followers of Jesus without regard to following the way Jews signified their allegiance to the Temple system. The issue was the appropriation of the atonement covenant standards to those who were not Jews and never a child of them. They didn't know what they were asking for!

Galatians 4:21: Tell me, you who want to be under law, do you not listen to the law? 22 For it is written that Abraham had two sons, one by the bondwoman and one by the free woman. 23 But the son by the bondwoman was born according to the flesh, and the son by the free woman through the promise. 24 This is allegorically speaking, for these [women] are two covenants: one [proceeding] from Mount Sinai bearing children who are to be slaves; she is Hagar. 25 Now this Hagar is Mount Sinai in Arabia and corresponds to the present Jerusalem, for she is in slavery with her children. 26 But the Jerusalem above is free; she is our mother. 27 For it is written, "REJOICE, BARREN WOMAN WHO DOES NOT BEAR; BREAK FORTH AND SHOUT, YOU WHO ARE NOT IN LABOR; FOR MORE NUMEROUS ARE THE CHILDREN OF THE DESOLATE THAN OF THE ONE WHO HAS A HUSBAND." 28 And you brethren, like Isaac, are children of promise. 29 But as at that time he who was born according to the flesh

*persecuted him [who was born] according to the Spirit,
so it is now also. 30 But what does the Scripture say?
"CAST OUT THE BONDWOMAN AND HER SON, FOR
THE SON OF THE BONDWOMAN SHALL NOT BE AN
HEIR WITH THE SON OF THE FREE WOMAN." 31 So
then, brethren, we are not children of a bondwoman, but
of the free woman. 5:1 It was for freedom that Christ set
us free; therefore keep standing firm and do not be
subject again to a yoke of slavery.*

If you read this the way I was taught to read it, **you would think
it said that the Torah was dispensed with in Jesus.** Yet, on
closer inspection, we have to understand that Jews didn't lump
all the Law together, and the covenant of Abraham was not the
same thing as the Law of Moses.

**The Abrahamic Covenant of God was the access agreement
to God through faith – long before the giving of the Law**.
Before Moses, it was by grace through faith in whatever
revelation God gave a man or woman. For Abraham it was the
promise of a son and then a nation. For Jacob, it was the reality
of a connection between Heaven and Earth in a stairway to
Heaven vision. After Moses, the way to access God's
satisfaction, as best the Word revealed it, was by coming under
the covenant of God with Israel and showing one's faith through
a series of specified actions that included Sabbath, circumcision
and celebration of sacrifices. To meet and follow God, a man
needed to **come to Judea** and hear of the God of Israel, and
serve Him. He needed to participate in the sacrificial system to
abate the wrath of God, while he believed all that God said in
His revealed truths of that day. That was what is termed the
FORMER COVENANT or OLD COVENANT.

From the Hebrew prophets (particularly those who declared the
future for the exiles) there emerged word that God would offer
Israel a NEW COVENANT whereby the whole of Israel at one
point in time would be completely saved and filled by God's spirit
(Jeremiah 31, Isaiah 59). On His way to doing that, God later

revealed that He would put blinders on Israel because of their sin (called the "shame" of the people, see Joel 1-2; Romans 10-11) and they would hear men of a foreign nation that would know their God when they did NOT know Him (Isaiah 28, Acts 2). When they heard the people of another tongue speaking truth, they would know their days of shame had begun. Yet, in the end, the New Covenant would release them from their shame, after it opened salvation to the world. The New Covenant had, in effect, **two stages** –

- One where the **Savior gave direct access to the world while Israel languished** largely in spiritual darkness.

- Another where **Israel is renewed at a time in the future when the times of the Gentiles are fulfilled** and God can renew the Jewish harvest.

In the beginning of the move from Old to New Covenant – there was strife as Jewish leaders wanted to co-opt any growth from Paul's movement to their own.

A battle ensued, and the Galatians were caught in the crossfire in a war of words. Paul called them to another picture:

- A Picture (4:21-26) Those who desire to follow the old atonement system, have you ever really read the Torah? Let me remind you of an old story…Abraham had two sons. One came from Hagar, but was not the one God gave in His promise. The other one came through His promise. This is like a picture of two covenants of God – one from Sinai, which enslaved people into continual sacrifice, pictured by the temple sacrifices and controls of the atonement system in Jerusalem. The other covenant is direct from Heaven - a freedom from that perpetual sacrifice, a direct connection of justification.

- A Point (4:27-28) The truth is like the song that calls for rejoicing among the outcasts – the direct adoption plan of Heaven will now yield vast fruits! They will be like Isaac – children of God's promise!

- A Parallel (4:29-5:1) The picture of Isaac being picked on by Ishmael is the picture we see today as those from Judea come to bind you who have been accepted by God through faith alone to an old system that has no power to save.

- A Plea (4:30-5:1) Throw them out the way Sarah cast out Hagar. You are children of Sarah, and they don't belong camping in your tent! Don't let them throw a yoke of continual sacrifice and Temple control over you, your calling is in Messiah as one free from all of that!

Paul essentially said this: Jerusalem on earth (with its atonement sacrifices run by Sanhedrin controllers) is at war with a spiritual Jerusalem in Heaven, where direct access to God is available through the now completed sacrifice of Jesus. The atonement system wants to dominate the direct access to God – and that is backwards. As you have patiently waded through this biblical debate with me, perhaps it is only fitting that we more closely connect the dots to where you and I live today. We aren't often debating whether Jewish leadership in Jerusalem should take control of the message of the local church. We haven't had a really good theological argument about killing bulls and goats for centuries. We don't really struggle with the notion of circumcision, and we don't check when you join the church – just so our visitors know. We meet on Sunday, and support Jewish groups that meet on Sabbath, along with non-Jewish mission points around the globe that do NOT. These issues seem distant and mind numbing to many – but they are not.

In a world that wants equality of value to mean that everyone must be made to do everything the same way - God has a response.

Both men and women are equal in value, but they are made to do different things. The stronger frame of most men was given to match their strong inner drive to protect a family and eventually become an elder in the community that protected the whole of the tribe with wisdom. As a general rule, men were better designed for war. Their bodies did not demand such painful cycles and they would never be called out of the line because they carried another human being within. Women were uniquely privileged to bear a child, while their man bore a spear, arrow, or sword. Putting women in combat isn't freeing them, it is creating an expectation they were not designed, on the whole, to carry. They stand in unique danger of molestation and misuse because we want them to see equality of value in equality of work – but **that is a mistake that will cost many of them dearly.** Agree with my illustration or not, that isn't my point. My point is that **God made people of equal value but didn't tell them all to do the same things in their walk with Him.** I can be a parent, but not bear a child. I can teach mixed audiences, but am not to teach young women in the quiet intimate settings that older women are to handle. I am equal to my wife, but I cannot do everything she is told to do as an experienced woman of God. That doesn't make me worth less – it makes me what I am called to be before my Creator.

In a time when tolerance replaces critical thinking and careful study regarding what God has said in His Word - God has a message.

We need to be careful not to sound defensive, but to defend truth. We need to be open to discussion, but unwilling to tread on the text for the sake of good feeling in the room. We need to walk a road with those with whom we acknowledge a disagreement, but we cannot, for the sake of peace and tranquility, sit still while those who are teaching false doctrines to our people are allowed to remain in our midst. They can come and worship with us, because the doors are publicly open. Yet, when they want a platform for teaching in this place, we will graciously, but pointedly, refuse them a voice.

One of the functions of teaching truth is spotting error – and that may offend some and may cause them to walk out the door. The longer I serve Jesus, the more I understand that there is a critical difference between someone who rejects me or my personality, and someone who refuses our message without carefully engaging the text. We live in a time with many self-ordained and self-proclaimed prophets. The substance of the argument is what must be deemed right or wrong, not the amount of belief in it. Lots of belief that eating pomegranates cures colon cancer won't make it so. It isn't the SIZE OF BELIEF; it is the OBJECT of it that makes it true or false.

It cannot be dismissed as a relic, nor ignored as a boring piece of literature. If it is God's Word, then it communicates God's message. If that message delineates differences between people – then it is what God said. No council of men should be able to dissuade us from our allegiance to God's message. No culture should wear down our sharp understanding of what it takes to please God.

In a **generation** that has sought to "dumb down" the harder process of deep thinking and careful research and replace it with platitude filled messages of personal comfort and repetitious songs with little substance – God has a **requirement**.

- We are required to study the Word that He has kept for us.
- We are required to answer the queries of life with His stated answers.
- No siren call of culture should convince us to call unimportant what He deems as important.
- Life planted in the womb, not by mere chemical process, but by the hand of a Creator, must be maintained as sacred.
- Marriage, not a contract between people, but a judicial joining in Heaven of a woman under the covering of a man, must be held as sacred.
- Worship of God must be maintained at the center of civic life for moral decisions to rule the day. These aren't options, and ignoring them has devastating consequences.

At the same time, we must recognize that truth isn't simple. Ask a calculus student – finding the answers can be complicated.

That doesn't mean they aren't true. God didn't try to reduce His Word to fortune cookie wisdom. **There is a need to study carefully, and to observe it wholly.** In the end, we see from a careful view of the Scripture...

God kept unique markers in place for the Jewish people that the church around the world need not be concerned about adopting, no matter what pressure they received to do so.

Dispelling Myths about the Gospel: Lessons in Galatians

Lesson Five: Galatians 5:1-13
"Myth Ten"

What does it REALLY mean to be FREE? The flag of the United States of America has been for generations a symbol of freedom all over the world. Its vibrant colors signify a land where a small group of men realized their dream for a government that has protected freedom of speech, freedom of religion, and freedom of the press as sacrosanct ideals. Those men prized these human freedoms so much that many were bankrupted or died defending them. Oddly enough, in the long history of man, there is no record before their document that recorded them all as God-given rights before the one penned by them. No one thought, in the ions of the past, those simple but vital freedoms were worth enshrining in a document, until this group of gentlemen farmers, shop keepers and tradesmen sat together to form a government that offered a profound statement of man's best intentions.

No sensible person would argue that these freedoms were not costly. At the same time, no thinking man or woman would deny these freedoms aren't absolute – they have limits. I may have free speech, but I cannot yell, "Fire!" in a public place no fire exists. I will be arrested if I claim to possess a bomb on a plane (even if there is no such device). Why is my free speech curtailed? The simple answer is that it is reined in by well-placed and defined limits. True freedom provides civil society protections by limiting personal freedoms only when failure to do so will cause significant harm to others. I have the right to disagree with you, but not to cheat you and swindle you out of your money. I have the right to articulate a contentious position, but not to alter the facts before a court of law or the Congress of the United States. At the same time, it is worth noting that civil freedom isn't the only realm in which freedom must be carefully defined.

Freedom has limits and freedom has rules. Freedom is not a "free for all" in behavior, but rather a state or environment that is made safe by appropriate limits. In fact, I want to make an observation. I believe that no one can successfully navigate the tough circumstances of life if they don't recognize that freedom has limits and rules, and we must learn to act within appropriate guidelines. We need to both learn the appropriate ground rules for interpersonal relationships, and regularly have a loving person hold us accountable for our actions. Today's redefinition of LOVE as TOLERANCE OF ALL BEHAVIOR is as weak as yesterday's definition of LOVE as LUST – so frequently stated on the radio of my youth. This fad will perhaps fade, but its thinking is enslaving the current generation into a kind of politically correct speech, while their uncivil behavior astoundingly increases but goes almost unabated. We need instruction, and we need correction.

The *Bible* defines freedom, and it makes clear how people who are free should use their liberty – especially that spiritual liberty found in Christ!

Key Principle: True freedom is found in intimate attachment to God initiated by faith in Christ alone, and lived out by careful diligence in following God's Spirit.

Because freedom in Christ isn't a trip to Outback with their famous motto "no rules" – we must challenge a spirit permeating the theology of the twenty-first century American church. There is a serious error that has been allowed to grow in our most hallowed halls, and some of it seems to stem from a misreading and misapplication of Galatians. It can be found in the misunderstanding of Paul's words at the beginning of Galatians

5 – it *"was for the sake of FREEDOM that Christ set us free!"* Yet, what he meant by this claim may NOT be what people use the statement to justify!

Paul made clear that Christ offered justification and freedom from the atonement system's bondage of continuous sacrifice – but it did not mean that believers were to devolve into undisciplined or loose living. To grasp his argument, we have to tear down some mythology, and then see what God really wanted us to become as a result of the truths about freedom He uncovered for us. Let's start with a myth that keeps popping up, as we lay to rest for one last time what Paul was, and was NOT saying about keeping the Law.

Myth 10: The Law is worthless (circumcision, etc.) **because no one can keep it!** If you break one law, it is as though you broke them all – so Jesus made it all pointless.

No matter where I go, I find people that use the verses at the beginning of Galatians 5 to justify practices that have little or nothing to do with Paul's argument. He wrote:

Galatians 5:1 It was for freedom that Christ set us free; therefore keep standing firm and do not be subject again to a yoke of slavery.

Before we go any further, let me say it clearly. Paul NEVER made this statement to justify ANY behavior that was morally forbidden in Scripture. Jesus didn't free us from the expectation before God that our walk of life would include immoral behavior, lying, cheating, stealing, disrespect of authority, immodesty, etc. For illustration purposes, you can see this kind of thinking in places like www.christianswingers.com, where you will be able to read:

Christian Swingers – New Dating Site for Faithful Couples: For Christian Swingers things are not easy – often other religious people judge you, out of ignorance or envy, telling you that your lifestyle and love practices are wrong. But the *Bible* teaches us, 'Judge not lest ye be judged' and there's that verse about the first stone... but if you're keen on keeping your privacy, well – yours, and don't want your friends, coworkers, other PTA members or just about anyone else to know that you don't have a problem with faith and enjoying free love with other couples, this site can help you! It's designed to cater to the needs of those like you: devout Christian couples who still want to have an active love life and share it with another, in good faith! ... Visit our club and discover other Christian couples with the same interests and desires who find you hot – Christian Swingers website will make your life easier and give you more access to potential dating partners!

Again, let me be clear. There is Christian, there is love, and there is freedom – but what these folks are talking about is neither free, nor Christian (Jesus didn't authorize a brothel nor visit one), nor is it love – it is spelled L-U-S-T. I know some of you may think this is a hoax, and that I am being extreme, but I assure you the changes that are happening are very real all around us, and the resistance of the church is growing extremely thin.

Let's get back to Scripture in Galatians 5:

Galatians 5:2 Behold I, Paul, say to you that if you receive circumcision, Christ will be of no benefit to you. 3 And I testify again to every man who receives circumcision that he is under obligation to keep the whole Law. 4 You have been severed from Christ, you who are seeking to be justified by law; you have fallen from grace. 5 For we through the Spirit, by faith, are waiting for the hope of righteousness. 6 For in Christ Jesus neither circumcision nor uncircumcision means anything, but faith working through love. 7 You were running well; who hindered you from obeying the truth? 8 This persuasion [did] not [come] from Him who calls you. 9 A little leaven leavens the whole lump [of dough].

10 I have confidence in you in the Lord that you will adopt no other view; but the one who is disturbing you will bear his judgment, whoever he is. 11 But I, brethren, if I still preach circumcision, why am I still persecuted? Then the stumbling block of the cross has been abolished. 12 I wish that those who are troubling you would even mutilate themselves. 13 For you were called to freedom, brethren; only [do] not [turn] your freedom into an opportunity for the flesh, but through love serve one another.

We have carefully explored the argument in the letter, whereby Paul reasoned that the sacrifice of Jesus on the cross alone provided the means to satisfy God and the old atonement system was finished and replaced. The freedom Paul spoke of in that context was NOT from the RULES OF THE BIBLE. However, we do have to answer some questions:

What WAS the issue here?

The entire argument of Galatians has been about the "formula of salvation, not a manifesto to get Jews to quit doing things God told them to do perpetually. Paul said based on everything we have seen (in Galatians 1-4), you should throw out those who are trying to place you under the thumb of the old atonement system (as he said at the end of Galatians 4). You should take a stand (*stay'-ko* — "stand fast, persevere") in the cancellation of the obligation (the word "free" is *eleutheróō* — properly "to be released from obligation or restriction") to the atonement law and those who run it in the Temple of Jerusalem. In short, Paul said, drop them, and don't feel any obligation to their beckoning to become enslaved by them or their teachings.

Paul moved on from his "drop them" to one final and clear statement about the defunct atonement system, He said:

Galatians 5:2 Behold I, Paul, say to you that if you receive circumcision, Christ will be of no benefit to you. 3 And I testify again to every man who receives circumcision that he is under obligation to keep the whole Law. 4 You have been severed from Christ, you who are seeking to be justified by law; you have fallen from grace.

Obviously, Paul didn't want Galatian Gentiles to start being circumcised. Why would circumcision (something God commanded Jews to do as a prerequisite for a walk with Him) suddenly hinder the work of Christ in the Galatians? Essentially, there are two reasons. **First**, God didn't tell GENTILES to do it. **Second**, if they started into the old and defunct system to please God, they would be drawn from the right way to satisfy God.

Imagine for a moment you are out west in a remote area. The last gas station you saw was more than an hour ago. You are on remote and winding mountain roads. The signs along the road are shot through with shotgun holes. The whitened skull of a bull is lying beside the road with the horns sticking out. As you drive, you pass over one old bridge after another – what appears to be the work of Roosevelt's WPA. There have been only slight repairs for years. As you come upon a curve, you see a fork in the road. The left side of the fork is blocked with old and deteriorating barricades. The right side of the fork is open for "traffic," but you are the only one you have seen along this road since you got on it. The closed side of the fork leads to the old main road, but was closed by the severing of a bridge that happened years before. The right side was the newer road, and it was open and safe to connect you to your destination... Now suppose you were being waved past the barriers into the broken road by someone who wanted to call you down the road to the broken highway, so that their gang could overtake you and get the benefit of your half tank of gas and the food items in your trunk..

Don't get confused about the actual argument Paul made...

It is clear that Paul was speaking about "salvation" or "justification" and not lifestyle issues after salvation (what theologians call "sanctification" issues). In 5:3, Paul makes a reference of circumcision as the "entry point" of the system of laws found in the Torah. Was he saying that circumcision was not appropriate for any believer because it forced the circumcised one into the keeping of the Law, be he Jew or Gentile? If that verse stood alone, or if it is quoted alone in an article or theological statement it could easily seem that way – but I would argue that is NOT what he is saying at all. In fact, if you keep reading, it becomes clear that Paul was concerned NOT about the practice of circumcision (something he has done to Timothy AFTER he led him to Christ for salvation (Acts 16:1-3), but about the ISSUE OF JUSTIFICATION, as he makes clear in 5:4.

Let me be exact in this: Paul wasn't destroying the value of a symbol of circumcision that God told Jews to do for *"all their generations"* (Genesis 17:12) at all. He was making clear that circumcision has ABSOLUTELY NO VALUE in the cause of satisfying God concerning a man's fallen condition, nor did the entire atonement system to which it belonged. In other words, Paul said circumcision had NO EFFECT on anyone's acceptance before God because of the full cleansing through faith in Jesus that replaced the former atonement system. I DON'T NEED circumcision to be saved, nor does my Jewish neighbor. At the same time, if my Jewish neighbor trusts Christ and stands in that alone for salvation, he is not exempted from doing those things God called on his people to do "for all their generations" if he cares about being obedient to God's Holy Word. He doesn't keep Sabbath or get circumcised to be saved – **he does those things God told his people to do BECAUSE he is saved and wants to honor the unique place God gave His people for all their generations,** looking to a future time when God will turn His eyes back to that nation. Along with that, he doesn't try to get those (i.e. Gentiles) who WEREN'T born under those commands of obedience to START keeping them.

Paul's distinction is clear: Jesus alone saves. After salvation, it matters what your IDENTITY was WHEN you were saved as to HOW you should walk. Sanctification is dependent upon God's assignment to you in your birth identity. How do I know? Paul made it clear in 1 Corinthians 7:

1 Corinthians 7:17 Only, as the Lord has assigned to each one, as God has called each, in this manner let him walk. And so I direct in all the churches. 18 Was any man called [when he was already] circumcised? He is not to become uncircumcised. Has anyone been called in uncircumcision? He is not to be circumcised. 19 Circumcision is nothing, and uncircumcision is nothing, but [what matters is] the keeping of the commandments of God. 20 Each man must remain in that condition in which he was called.

The distinction between those who were called to salvation in Christ as Gentiles and those who were called to salvation in Christ as Jews was to be maintained after salvation in daily life. Jews and Gentiles became ONE in Messiah's salvation, but they were as distinct in lifestyle as bondmen and free men, as men and women. Each had restrictions and parameters of service, and these were determined by where God placed them in society when they came to Christ. In a unique distinction from the others on the list, bondmen (slaves) were encouraged to take advantage of any legal way to change their estate if an opportunity was presented (1 Corinthians 7:21).

As a result of all this detail, what we know is that Paul was arguing that circumcision has no effect on salvation whatsoever, regardless of WHO you are, where you come from, or what your background has been. **At the same time, Paul wasn't trying to get Jews to STOP following the commands of God to the Jewish people.** The book of Acts makes clear that Paul was concerned that people who thought such things about him be corrected by a public display. Do you recall the scene? Paul returned from his third mission journey. He arrived in Jerusalem, and the believers were EXCITED, but there was a murmur in the room. Let me remind you of the story from Acts 21, as Dr. Luke, the writer, reminds us.

Acts 21:17 After we arrived in Jerusalem, the brethren received us gladly. 18 And the following day Paul went in with us to James and all the elders were present. 19 After he had greeted them, he [began] to relate one by one the things which God had done among the Gentiles through his ministry. 20 And when they heard it they [began] glorifying God; and they said to him, "You see, brother, how many thousands there are among the Jews of those who have believed, and they are all zealous for the Law; 21 and they have been told about you, that you are teaching all the Jews who are among the Gentiles to forsake Moses, telling them not to circumcise their children nor to walk according to the customs. 22 "What, then, is [to be done]? They will certainly hear that you have come."

Paul didn't defend that he was doing any such teaching – to get Jews to stop keeping the things God told them to do forever, but took a public vow to show THAT HE WAS NOT teaching Jews to stop circumcising. He was not saying, "Jews are OUT and church is IN". He was not exclaiming, "Law BAD, grace GOOD." He was NOT just placating Jewish sentiment for the sake of making them happy. If that is true, Paul was a political animal, not to be trusted because he wrote one thing to the Galatians, and lived the opposite before the Judeans. That isn't Dr. Luke's view, and that isn't a true retelling of the story – but it IS the popular mythology in a great many church circles.

Look back at Galatians 5. Paul talked about JUSTIFICATION in 5:4, and connected it with CIRCUMCISION. Since circumcision started long before the atonement system was defined in the

Torah, why did Paul connect circumcision with the sacrificial system?

To a Jew, circumcision was *part* of the sacrificial system.

It didn't START there, but it eventually became indelibly linked to it. Some *Bible* students struggle to reconcile how the issue of circumcision has ANYTHING TO DO WITH the issue of sin satisfaction or atonement. They may have trouble making the connection in their mind that would not have been troubling for Paul, or any educated Jew. The reason is simple: **In the sacrificial system, only circumcised people could fully participate**. In places like Exodus 12 – the famous passage on the Passover, God said:

Exodus 12:48 But if a stranger sojourns with you, and celebrates the Passover to the LORD, let all his males be circumcised, and then let him come near to celebrate it; and he shall be like a native of the land. But no uncircumcised person may eat of it.

During the days of the atonement system, the "ticket in" to be able to be a part of the Israelite system of sacrifice under the first temple system was circumcision. By the time of the second temple, (what many call the NT Period), there were two kinds of "proselytes" to Judaism – a proselyte of "righteousness" and a "proselyte of the gate." The term "proselyte" is from an ancient Greek term for "stranger" or "newcomer." Rabbinic Judaism separated them into two types: *ger tzedek* "proselytes of righteousness" and *ger toshav* "resident proselyte, proselytes of the gate, limited proselyte, half-proselyte").

- A ger tsedek was a gentile who came under the covenant God had with the Jewish people in the atonement system and was bound to all the doctrines and precepts of the Torah, considered a full member of the Jewish people. They were circumcised as adults and immersed in a *mikvah* "a bath for ritual cleansing" in order to participate in the system of sacrifice.

- A ger toshav was a resident alien who lived among the Jews in Judea and was learning to follow the Torah, but were not required to be circumcised nor keep all the Torah commands. They were bound to the Noahide Laws (do not idolatry, worship idols, blaspheme, murder, commit biblically immoral sexual acts, steal, etc.) to be assured of a place in the world to come. One NT *ger toshav* was likely the centurion Cornelius (Acts 10:22) who was referred to as a "God fearing man." Another was likely the "Ethiopian Eunuch" (Acts 8) who could not be fully embraced in the Temple because of his deformity (Deuteronomy. 23:1).

Paul made clear the entry to a defunct system was no help for salvation, and allowing the people who are offering this confusion to stay would only hurt them:

Galatians 5:5 For we, through the Spirit by faith, are waiting for the hope of righteousness. 6 For in Christ Jesus neither circumcision nor uncircumcision means anything, but faith working through love. 7 You were running well; who hindered you from obeying the truth? 8 This persuasion [did] not [come] from Him who calls you. 9 A little leaven leavens the whole lump [of dough].

Paul was SO DISTURBED by the people pulling them off track, he spoke rather graphically and in effect said in Galatians 5:12 "I wish that those who are troubling you would even mutilate themselves. If they are SO BENT on getting you to do this, **let them cut themselves!"**

Jesus didn't make the Law pointless – he made the sacrifices pointless. He didn't strip the symbol of circumcision from the Jewish people. He put it back in the category of unique identity commands and cut it away from anything that was required by God for justification of ANYONE and for practice of Gentiles under any circumstances. Jews can do it to show they are Jews, but not to get to Heaven. Gentiles shouldn't feel pressured to do it at all – since it is meaningless in their direct access to God.

SO WHAT?

I have poured out, in exacting detail, a passage that is used to open the door to countless permissions of bad behavior among believers. The "liberty in Jesus" is cited often in debates where people decide that rules of behavior of any type have been eliminated in the "destruction of the law" by Paul – a wholly misunderstood approach to God's Word.

Let's be clear: **God's limits aren't bondage – the sacrificial system's incompletion was**. Liberty isn't a release to engage in moral filth that which God forbade people of the past to do – it was the freedom to directly access an intimate and personal relationship with God through belief in Christ and His saving blood. Practicing a symbol God gave people to do for their unique and enduring identity wasn't a description of some "cultural practice" – it was a description of God's command to Abraham repeated over and over as a measurable symbol of identity. Paul wasn't arguing to chop out parts of the *Bible* or become complacent in following God completely – he was making a distinction between the formula of salvation and the distinctive forms of sanctification.

Paul never argued that the life of a follower of God was marked by never denying any physical desire. He never meant by "yoke" that the Law was the problem – only that it couldn't provide, even in the scores of animal sacrifices – a permanent and complete solution to sin.

Listen to the subtle way this is confused: David Guzik, a commentator of enduringword.com wrote, If you become circumcised, Christ will profit you nothing: When we embrace the law as **our rule of walking with God,** we must let go of Jesus.

He is no longer our righteousness; we attempt to earn it ourselves.

That is dangerous speech in its implications, and it *wasn't* Paul's argument. If it were, he needed to apologize for the confusion he made to that very point in Jerusalem in Acts 21. Paul didn't want people to strip an allegiance to living life according to the standards of the many books of the *Bible* that preceded his writing career. What he wanted to do was clarify that the atonement system was broken and replaced. That is about justification, not about whether "doing the things God's Word teaches in the first half are cancelled in the second half."

I want to deliberately defend Jewish believers who keep Sabbath and are improperly called LEGALISTS – Paul called them JEWISH BELIEVERS. If that isn't true – he should have corrected the people in Jerusalem who knew Christ and yet were "zealous to keep the Law – but he didn't correct them, he joined with them (Acts 21). They were saved by the cross and lived as believers by the standards God gave to their fathers.

- Legalists aren't people who DO what God told them to do – they are called "obedient" in the Bible. They become wrong when they apply those rules to ANOTHER PEOPLE not given the rules.

- Legalism isn't having rules – it is misapplying God's placement of them for the purpose of gaining control of another's actions.

Paul closed the section with an admonition in *Galatians 5:13: For you were called to freedom, brethren; only [do] not [turn] your freedom into an opportunity for the flesh, but through love serve one another.*

The freedom from the continual sacrifices of the atonement and all the labor that goes along with it was not given to us so that we may release ourselves to inattention to our walk with God, nor waste our stewardship on personal extravagance – it was a unique opportunity to allow us through our walk with Jesus to serve one another.

The point of the Law was not to destroy one another by consuming each other in the arguments over the law. When we do, we are adopting standards without the objective they were ever intended to produce – a community! When those who were never given the Law try to make it the standard in their lives (to become a new version of the Jewish people) they corrupt the binding influence the Spirit of God should have on their lives – to bind them to each other and to help them consistently be pleasing to God.

If you allow the Spirit to lead you in your relationships, you will follow all that Jesus is concerned about for your building a community as Gentile believers. You will see the flesh without learning every careful distinction of the Law. There are many who live godly lives without a thorough knowledge of the Law – with little desire to keep it. **The following of the Spirit should produce bonds that will not come with angry disputing and boasting!**

We will need to revisit this passage to look more closely, now that the atonement argument is finished. You have been patient through all of this. I wonder if, in all the words of Galatians 5, you see the clear point of the end of the chapter. God had a goal with the Law, and it is the SAME GOAL that He has with His Spirit's leading – to produce a loving, active, vibrant corps of people that live joyfully for Him!

I want to close this lesson with a It comes in the form of a story, but it really IS a plea.

Harry Houdini, the famed escape artist, issued a challenge wherever he went. He could be locked in any jail cell in the country, he claimed, and set himself free quickly and easily.

Always he kept his promise, but one time something went wrong. Houdini entered the jail in his street clothes; the heavy, metal doors clanged shut behind him. He took from his belt a concealed piece of metal, strong and flexible. He set to work immediately, but something seemed to be unusual about this lock. For 30 minutes, he worked and got nowhere. An hour passed, and still he had not opened the door. By now, he was bathed in sweat and panting in exasperation, but he still could not pick the lock. Finally, after laboring for 2 hours, Harry Houdini collapsed in frustration and failure against the door he could not unlock. However, when he fell against the door, it swung open! It had never been locked at all! But in his mind it was locked and that was all it took to keep him from opening the door and walking out of the jail cell... I plead with you to stop struggling with ANY LIST that you think keeps you from God. Open the cage. Jesus unlocked it. There is no longer condemnation for those who trust His completed work. If you think you need to earn God's love, you haven't checked the cage door. It is now unlocked.

I plead with you to stop struggling with ANY LIST that you think keeps you from God. Open the cage. Jesus unlocked it. There is no longer condemnation for those who trust His completed work. If you think you need to earn God's love, you haven't checked the cage door. It is now unlocked. **Come on out!**

True freedom is found in intimate attachment to God initiated by faith in Christ alone, and lived out by careful diligence in following God's Spirit.

Dispelling Myths about the Gospel: Lessons in Galatians

Lesson Six: Galatians 5:14-26
"Myth Eleven"

When you went out on the road this morning, you probably didn't observe some things in the world around you that have a PROFOUND EFFECT on your day. On my drive each morning, I see neighbors walking their dogs (and a few dogs walking my neighbors!) Some people are manicuring their lawns, cutting, raking, cleaning, edging and the like. I may pass some joggers, bicycle enthusiasts and walkers who are out and about to exercise their bodies and get some fresh air. Driving down the road, I will no doubt encounter some of our world-class Floridian drivers – people who seem to want to make the point that no one should put stress on the engine by actually depressing the gas pedal.

One of the interesting parts of that daily journey is that it MASKS a problem. You and I have encountered an issue so frequently along the way we may not even see it. We pass by unaware, because we have grown accustomed to the world around us.

Here is a thought: Every person you passed today was a DUI – driving under the influence of SOMETHING. Though each person got out of bed with his own idea about what he wanted to accomplish, he, is, in fact, being "driven" by inner desires, ideas and influences that were pressing him to act on his plans for the day. According to the *Bible,* everyone is being driven by something. Most of the people we meet in the world are under the influence of the flesh – simply doing the things that make sense to them, because they are following a variety of hungers and desires the world would call "natural". Of course, a significant problem with that "natural" view is that it underestimates and even ignores the truth that after the Fall in the Garden, man's nature was marred, and so were his natural desires. When the umbilical cord that connected the life flow of God's Spirit in them was cut in an act of mutiny – a state was initiated that is referred to in the Bible as being "dead" in spirit – with no particular connection to their Creator. The *Bible* refers back to that time as the "fall of the flesh" and presents fallen man as alive in body, but estranged from God and His purposes.

If you look further into the Bible, it cautions that others around us – the vast majority – are equally dead in spirit, and have been placed under the domination of the prince of the power of the air – the enemy of the Creator. The *Bible* refers to these people as "under the world's system" – a temporary state in which rebellion against God and reliance on self looks completely normal. In that system, God is a crutch made up by weaker men, while self-reliance is touted as maturity. When the *Bible* mentions things like "love not the world, nor the things in it" – this influence is being mentioned. We are not called to eschew cute puppies and force ourselves not to enjoy a sunset. That isn't the "world" about which the *Bible* is speaking. The world system is a fallen system that operates in a perpetual state of rebellion that is so common and so entrenched, it looks completely normal this side of the Garden of Eden's mutiny.

Look even deeper, and you will find religious people who are "under the influence of the law" – deeply committed to their daily actions because of something they believe to be the "right thing to do" (moral and religious obligation), in spite of the fact that they have no real attachment to their Creator or His purpose for them. These are people who follow the tradition of their religion and hope God thinks they are fine because they are faithful to that tradition. Their religion brings them comfort in this life, even if it has no effect on the next. God doesn't offer truth, then put value on the shades of false thinking. He sent His Son to provide a bridge to God, and because of that is not particularly open to other ways people are trying to erect their own bridge. Every religious effort is an attempt to cross the chasm of separation in a way that ignores God's sacrifice – another expression of rebellious self-reliance. Still, many are being driven by an influence of religious fervor – especially if you drive on Sunday morning.

In contrast, there are a few (and on Sunday morning, perhaps more people than usual) that the *Bible* says are being led through life under the dominating influence of God's Spirit. Their lives are reflecting the fruit of the connection to God.

We want to move in close and see how they do that, and discover how our own lives can be pulled into that way of living. We will talk about people who are **DOMINATED BY THE SPIRIT OF GOD**. Even more, we want to examine what they are. Let's review two truths we have seen many times, just to make sure we are on the "same page:"

First, here are two kinds of people in the world - those who know God and those who need to know Him. We mean by this there are those who have a personal relationship with God through Jesus, and there are those God desires to come to that place.

Second, there are two kinds of believers in the world - those who are honestly attempting to allow God's Spirit to dominate them and those who need to start or re-start doing that. By this, we mean that there are those in relationship with Jesus who are not allowing God's Spirit to direct them, but are making their own choices of direction in daily life. They know Jesus as Savior, but they don't let Him control their goals, choices, etc. because they claim the position of their own lordship in relation to their choices.

Cutting through all the clutter, it seems the defining difference between the two believers is really one issue – their effort to surrender or their choice to keep leading themselves. The last portion of Galatians 5 deals with that in succinct terms.

Key Principle: The mature believer learns to let the empowering of the Spirit bear the fruit of the Spirit. He isn't interested in trying to do what doesn't honor the Savior in the name of freedom.

In our series on "myths" of the Gospel – popular sentiments that are NOT true, there is an eleventh myth that keeps "popping up" in daily life…

Myth 11: The Law is simply now to love! All that detail does you no good, because it all has been distilled in Jesus to "Love your neighbor."

Galatians 5:13: For you were called to freedom, brethren; only [do] not [turn] your freedom into an opportunity for the flesh, but through love serve one another. 14 For the whole Law is fulfilled in one word, in the [statement], "YOU SHALL LOVE YOUR NEIGHBOR AS YOURSELF." 15 But if you bite and devour one another, take care that you are not consumed by one another. 16 But I say, walk by the Spirit, and you will not carry out the desire of the flesh. 17 For the flesh sets its desire against the Spirit, and the Spirit against the flesh; for these are in opposition to one another, so that you may not do the things that you please. 18 But if you are led by the Spirit, you are not under the Law. 19 Now the deeds of the flesh are evident, which are: immorality, impurity, sensuality, 20 idolatry, sorcery, enmities, strife, jealousy, outbursts of anger, disputes, dissensions, factions, 21 envying, drunkenness, carousing, and things like these, of which I forewarn you, just as I have forewarned you, that those who practice such things will not inherit the kingdom of God. 22 But the fruit of the Spirit is love, joy, peace, patience, kindness, goodness, faithfulness, 23 gentleness, self-control; against such things there is no law. 24 Now those who belong to Christ Jesus have crucified the flesh with its passions and desires. 25 If we live by the Spirit, let us also walk by the Spirit. 26

Let us not become boastful, challenging one another, envying one another.

Did Jesus really wipe out any need for me to deliberately make efforts to deal with my daily walk before God? Some people think so. The pop version of Christian freedom seems to be that we can choose to do whatever we want as a child of God – because Jesus took away all moral obligation to DO anything to be pleasing to God.

Here is the problem: Jesus provided "JUDICIAL SATISFACTION" for our sin, paying completely for all of it. For the follower of Jesus who has placed his or her faith in Christ alone for salvation, we don't get into Heaven through any effort we make on any level. Our door pass was completely made possible by Jesus and His sacrifice. The problem is, many believers stop thinking clearly at that point. Entry to God's Kingdom may be fully paid, but Look at Paul's instruction to the Galatian believers:

Galatians 5:13: For you were called to freedom, brethren; only [do] not [turn] your freedom into an opportunity for the flesh, but through love serve one another.

The question behind the statement:

Paul opens with a response to a simple question: **"What is the full purpose of our freedom in Christ?"** Was the relationship to God through Jesus' sacrifice ONLY about our eternal destiny as individuals, or Paul argued in the first part of the chapter that the point of the Law of God in the Torah was not for God's people to destroy one another by consuming each other in the arguments over the Law. It was costly and time consuming to obey the Torah standards that marked atonement law. Without the need to raise a lamb for sacrifice, without the requirement to go before God with constant sin offerings – religious life just got a whole lot simpler and cheaper. The problem is, that isn't true.

Failure to do so was, in effect, adopting standards without the objective they were ever intended to produce. Paul continued:

Galatians 5:14: For the whole Law is fulfilled in one word, in the [statement], "YOU SHALL LOVE YOUR NEIGHBOR AS YOURSELF." 15 But if you bite and devour one another, take care that you are not consumed by one another. 16 But I say, walk by the Spirit, and you will not carry out the desire of the flesh.

The Law was given for more than making one right before God – it was for community formation. It was to bring about peace, long life and deep relationships between people. Moses wrote as much in Deuteronomy 6, but many seemed to have forgotten that part. Harming one another was unlawful, unloving, and outside the character of one who truly wanted to serve God with all their heart. Paul made the point that even in freedom from the atonement law – the same is still true. God wants people who not only VALUE SALVATION but in daily practice VALUE EACH OTHER in relationship. Paul then made clear a warning: when we follow the Spirit, we do that which is unnatural to the fallen man and his flesh.

A spirit-filled life is a disciplined life – not a lazy "do what is natural" life. It is to behavioral choices what diet and exercise are to anyone who desires to train for successful athletic performance. Though I am born of the Spirit, I have much of the value system of fallen man still coaching my thinking – and it must be dealt with by God's Spirit through God's Word. Flesh wars against spirit like a disciplined diet wars against a hungry stomach.

Here is the truth: **I don't WANT to discipline my life. I want to SLEEP IN when I should get up. I want to eat WHAT I WANT, WHEN I WANT – and let's not even TALK about exercise**. When you think about the Spirit-filled life, it ISN'T an excuse for laziness – but it is a battle against flesh thinking that CAN BE

WON because the Spirit lives WITHIN ME! Look again at verse 16: "But I say, walk by the Spirit, and you will not carry out the desire of the flesh." Obviously, walking by the Spirit is something that I CAN do, and something that can be measured by whether or not I am living "under the influence" of satiating the desires of the flesh.

What is the Spirit-Filled Walk?

Paul elsewhere makes the claim that "Now, the Lord is the Spirit; and where the Spirit of the Lord is there is liberty or freedom" (2 Corinthians 3:6, 17). He says that because the Spirit of the Lord is in us, we are now free to walk with Him without any constraints. We are free moral agents when it comes to pleasing God. We are released from allegiance to perpetual sin (Romans 6 makes this argument completely), and we are no longer compelled to walk according to the flesh as we were before the Spirit of God was planted inside us and God was completely satisfied with us having put on the righteousness found in Jesus.

> **First**, note in verse sixteen that **walking by the Spirit's direction is not passive**. The issue isn't simply talking about walking in the Spirit, or sitting in the Spirit – it is making my life choices form the pattern of a walk.

> **Second**, note that **walking by the Spirit is not running**. It isn't achieved through endless, exhausting activity. It isn't about harder work for God so that we will become more spiritual.

> **Third**, note in 5:17, that **walking by God's Spirit isn't a license to indulge my leftover fallen natural desires**. Paul could not have said it more clearly.

Galatians 5:17: For the flesh sets its desire against the Spirit, and the Spirit against the flesh; for these are in opposition to one another, so that you may not do the things that you please.

A lecturer was once invited to speak to a religion class at a private high school on the topic of Christianity. At the end of his talk, an athletic-looking, street-wise student raised his hand and asked, "Do you have a lot of don't in your church?" Sensing that the student had a deeper motive, he answered, "What you really want to ask me is if we have any freedom, right?" "Yes," he nodded. "Sure, I'm free to do whatever I want to do," he answered. The student's face reflected his disbelief at what the man said. "I'm free to rob a bank. But I'm mature enough to realize that I would be in bondage to that act for the rest of my life. I'd have to cover up my crime, go into hiding or eventually pay for what I did. I'm also free to tell a lie. But if I do, I have to keep telling it and I have to remember who I told it to and how I told it or I will get caught. I'm free to do drugs, abuse alcohol, and live a sexually immoral life-style. All of those "freedoms" lead to bondage. I'm free to make those choices, but considering the consequences, would you really be free?"

If I were speaking to that student, I think I would have continued to make yet one more point. The issue of freedom is that I can now please God in my daily choices, and that is something a mature believer should HUNGER TO DO.

Babies care about themselves to the exclusion of others. They cry when they are hungry to get you to FEED THEM. They fuss about a wet diaper because they don't have the ability to relieve the discomfort without your help. All of us get older, and some of us GROW UP. "Growing up" literally means "seeing past MY NEEDS" and looking to the benefit of others.

> **Fourth**, if you look closely at 5:18, it is clear that **walking by the Spirit isn't simply mimicking the laws God gave in the past**. In fact, it is more complex than that. Walking by the Spirit is accomplished when I recognize the principles behind God's laws of the past – identifying what God really cared about in each situation.

Paul said in *Galatians 5:18*, *"But if you are led by the Spirit, you are not under the Law"* **for at least two reasons:**

First, People from Judea were telling them the way to walk with God was to walk in the Law – but that was shortsighted. The issue wasn't simply: "What did God say to the Jewish followers of the past" – but the much more complex, "What does an unchanging God truly care about?" as revealed in those past situations. The new situations of people as they spread across the globe would have pulled the Law apart. After all, it wasn't possible by the time of Paul for EVERY JEW to go to Jerusalem three times a year from everywhere they lived, in spite of Deuteronomy 16:16. It isn't possible to keep a sacrifice without a temple – so parts of the Law were forcibly suspended by circumstance.

Second, The freedom of following God is found in the insertion of His Divine standards inside the human heart, and God uses inner transformation as the modus operandi of the whole New Covenant, just as He promised Israel in Jeremiah 31. That is a BETTER PLAN! Telling someone that it's wrong to do this or that doesn't give them the power to stop doing it!

The War Within

Look at the WAR WITHIN YOU as a believer for a minute. In Galatians 5:19-21, God makes clear the works of the flesh are all ABOUT ME taking care of ME (at least my perceived needs). Here we have a list of fifteen deeds we can be drawn into – all of which displease God and enslave us:

- Immorality: *porneia*: "illicit sexual activity or intercourse," or essentially using the body for self-pleasures without regard to the proper use of the gift of sexuality.

- Impurity: *akatharsia*: "uncleansed living, living with unbridled desires that are not corrected." This is literally about living in a withdrawn state from God, because you refuse to yield to His cleansing and have the relationship restored. It is hiding in guilt and isolation from God, because you don't want to stop doing what you are doing.

One of the shocking things about the day in which we live is the arrogance, sheer aggressiveness and verbosity of those walking in sinful practices...

There is an old story about how a mountain lion felt so good after eating an entire bull, he started roaring. He kept it up until a hunter tracked the sound and shot him... The moral of that story: When you're full of bull, keep your mouth shut.

- Sensuality: *aselgia*: "shameless hungers for self-fulfillment." We see this in people who openly make life about their pleasure and walk about thinking that way of seeing life is fine with God! Today, a great many Christians are in fact, sensual thinkers.

- Idolatry: *idolateria*: "things pertaining to idols or unbridled desire for money." Anything that comes between you and a relationship of intimacy with God is considered an idol.

- Sorcery: *farmakia*: " use of anesthetizing drugs or 'highs' from them." This is a byproduct of the immature person who needs to constantly feel good without regard for the effects of their behavior on themselves or others.

- Enmities: *echthros*: "someone openly hostile and energized by deep-seated hatred." It implies irreconcilable hostility, with actions prompted by envy or hatred.

- Strife: *eris*: "wrangling and dissention." This is the notion that causing troubles between people will reposition me into a better place in the relationship with one of them.

- Jealousy: *zelos*: "to want what has not been granted to you." We involve ourselves in this when we obsess over things that we don't possess that others seem to have.

- Outbursts of anger: *thoomus*: "boiling over passionate lashing out verbally or physically." We buy into this when we claim to be a victim of our own emotions, as in: "It's not my fault; they all make me so mad!"

- Disputes: *erithia*: "electioneering, manipulation for personal gain." This is using people so that we can get what we want out of them, without regard for their intrinsic value.

- Dissentions: *dikhosetia*: "to force a wedge between to divide."

- Factions: *haheresis*: "factions like Pharisees or Sadducees that operated to undercut each other without regard to those wounded in the process." It is what happens when we believe our point is more important than the other person is!

- Envying: *fthonos*: "to plot the downfall because of jealousy." This is a product of jealousy, with the mixture of revenge, as in: "You are going down sister!"

- Drunkeness: *methay*: "intoxication." This is a life that buys into a lie that "I can't face my problems" and settles for the dulling effects.

- Carousing: *komos*: from the Bacchus festival; "late night revelries that include boisterous displays." This is a demonstration of the modern epicurean motto: "Life is short and I want to have as much fun as I can!"

All of these items are about ME.

- **My Pleasure**
- **My Happiness**
- **My Satisfaction**
- **My Needs**
- **My Wants**

Each stands in direct contrast to the "other person centered" lifestyle taught in the Scriptures. I want to be very clear so that you will be equipped to understand the changing sounds in the world around you. As biblical influence wanes in our society, the understanding of maturity and adulthood is also changing. What the *Bible* makes clear as "infantile behavior," the world will increasingly laud as "adult behavior." Here are places you will see this trend:

- Youths cannot be denied their desire to have sex when they feel it is appropriate. God's Word: It isn't right unless it is within the context God says it is supposed to happen, period. Any other approach will rob the picture of intimacy, break the proper bonds of the family, and add disease, weakness and affliction to our society. Both physical health and mental health needs will increase.

- Advertising everything with sensual and sexual overtones is increasingly thought of as both "appropriate and normal." There are commercials for everything from fragrances to underwear that would have been deemed pornographic just a short time ago.

- Competitors are routinely stealing blue prints, formulas, and even whole product lines as it begins to sound like the "rough and tumble of today's business." Really? We used to call it "theft."

- Lie to people to get them to buy into your legislation. Some people will call it "smart politics." We used to call it simply "telling lies."

Dispelling Myths about the Gospel: Lessons in Galatians

- When people include beer bashes as a "natural part" of college life, they surrender the argument that adulthood is about building controls on your own away from parents.

Note the end of this selfish shopping list.

Paul wrote at the end of *Galatians 5:21: ...which I forewarn you, just as I have forewarned you, that those who practice such things will not inherit the kingdom of God.*

Look at those words. Paul claimed that **ACTIONS AND BEHAVIORS could show the reality of a person's true walk with God.** Today's American Christian all too often wants nothing to do with that kind of thinking. In a world centered on individual rights and liberties almost to the exclusion of community responsibility, this is foreign thinking. This shocking claim is that **there is, in fact, a connection between how I live and whether or not I truly belong to Jesus Christ and His Kingdom.** Let that soak in for a moment. Paul actually claims that those who love Jesus and trust Him as their Savior will make different choices than they did before they knew Him.

The *Bible* teacher inside me won't let this go without a question: Is that true of YOUR LIFE? Are you consciously asking God to help you walk differently than you did in your old life choices before you knew Jesus?

A Fresh Wind

At this point in the letter, Paul lifts up the readers. He reminds them that God imparted His Spirit to us, and give us a breath of fresh air in the reminder of God's work in us. He offered a picture of the life "produce" of one dominated by the Spirit of God.

Galatians 5:2: But the fruit of the Spirit is love, joy, peace, patience, kindness, goodness, faithfulness, 23 gentleness, self-control; against such things there is no law. 24 Now those who belong to Christ Jesus have crucified the flesh with its passions and desires. 25 If we live by the Spirit, let us also walk by the Spirit.

Paul reminded the Galatians that following the Spirit wouldn't put them in conflict with the Law of God – it would help them see the principles of that Law clearly. Look at the nine fruits that are perhaps quite familiar to *Bible* students:

- Love: *agape*: "acting to meet needs of others without expectation of personal benefit."

- Joy: *kharah*: "the resolute assurance of God's recognition."

- Peace: *iraynay*: "confident rest in God's promises."

- Patience: *makrothumia*: "distant boiling." A transportation safety report suggests that the annual of people running red lights in the United States is reported to be about seven billion dollars. The average amount of time saved by running a red light is 50 seconds.

- Kindness: *kray-stot-ace*: "akin to moral integrity." It comes from a potter's word for "in usable condition."

- Goodness: *agathós:* "inherently (intrinsically) good;" as to the believer, the term describes what originates from God and is empowered by Him in their life, through faith.

- Faithfulness: *pistis*: "living by the vision of what God says is true;" a biblical worldview.

  Norman Geisler, as a child, went to a VBS because he was invited by some neighbor children. He went back to the same church for Sunday School classes for 400

Sundays. Each week he was faithfully picked up by a bus driver. Week after week, he attended church, but never made a commitment to Christ. Finally, during his senior year in High School, after being picked up for church over 400 times, he did commit his life to Christ. What if that bus driver had given up on Geisler at 395? What if the bus driver had said, "This kid is going nowhere spiritually, why waste any more time on him?" (Max Lucado, *God Came Near*, Multnomah Press, 1987, p. 133)

• Gentleness: *pra-ootace*: "mild disposition, meekness (or "gentle strength") which expresses power with reserve and measure."

• Self-control: *engratia*: "master one's own desires." Plato used the term as "self-mastery." It is the spirit that has mastered its desires and its love of pleasure. It is used of the athlete's discipline of his body (1 Corinthians 9:25) and of the Christian's mastery of sex (1 Corinthians 7:9).

Secular Greek uses it of the virtue of an emperor who never lets his private interests influence the government of his people. It is the virtue that makes a man so master of himself that he is fit to be the servant of others. (William Barclay). He further states: Self-control is that great quality which comes to a man when Christ is in his heart, that quality which makes him able to live and to walk in the world, and yet to keep his garments unspotted from the world.

It is akin to Proverbs 25:28 (GWT) Like a city broken into is a person who lacks self-control, left without a wall.

John Maxwell writes: In reading about the lives of great people, I found that the first victory they won was over themselves.

There was an office sign that read: If you could kick the person responsible for most of your troubles, you wouldn't be able to sit for a week.

Former *Tonight Show* host Jack Paar stated: Looking back, my life seems to be one long obstacle course, with me as the chief obstacle.

The Antidote Offers Healing

Look at these words of Scripture from *Galatians 5. 24: Now those who belong to Christ Jesus have crucified the flesh with its passions and desires.*

Paul makes the BOLD CLAIM through the Spirit's initiation of the text claiming: If we truly belong to Jesus, He has provided in HIS BLOOD the empowering to DIE TO SELF. One man's blood injected righteousness and power to conquer the selfish fever.

Gordon Curley offered this story from the twentieth century that may help illustrate this point:

In 1927, in West Africa, a blood specimen was taken from a native man named Asibi, who was sick with yellow fever. A vaccine was made from the original strain of virus obtained from this man. In fact, all the vaccine manufactured since 1927 by the Rockefeller Foundation and health agencies derives from the original strain of virus obtained from this one man. Carried down to the present day from one laboratory to another, through repeated cultures and by enormous multiplication, it has offered immunity to yellow fever to millions of people in many countries. Through the creative imagination of science, the blood of this one man in West Africa has been made available to serve the whole human race. In another, more important way, the blood of another Man has been made to serve the human race.

Here is the truth: **You don't have to serve the flesh; you have been injected with Jesus and His Spirit**. Now the real question... **What will you DO with that information?**

The mature believer isn't interested in trying to do what doesn't honor the Savior in the name of freedom, but learns to let the empowering of the Spirit bear the fruit of the Spirit.

Dispelling Myths about the Gospel:
Lessons in Galatians

Lesson Seven: Galatians 6:1-18
"Myth Twelve"

Most of us truly enjoy being together with our family at the holiday season – but apparently, we don't represent all of modern American society. I searched the blogosphere a few days back, and apparently, the family gatherings of a significant number of Americans are froth with danger and apprehension. Martha Beck wrote for Oprah Winfrey's online magazine these words:

In the Uncle Remus story of the tar baby, Brer Rabbit picks a fight with a lifelike doll made out of tar and turpentine. The tar baby is so gluey that when the rabbit punches it, his fists get hopelessly stuck. He tries to kick his way free trapping his feet, then finishes off with an infuriated head butt that renders him utterly helpless. I can't think of a more fitting metaphor for family life in the 21st century. There's nothing in the world as sticky as a dysfunctional family. You can put half your life's savings into therapy—good therapy, effective therapy—and, 15 minutes into a holiday reunion, you still become hopelessly enmeshed in the same old crazy dynamics. Your assertiveness training goes out the window the minute your brother begins his traditional temper tantrum. A mere sigh from your grandmother triggers an attack of codependency so severe you end up giving her your house. For many people, family get-togethers require strategies for staying out of such sticky situations.

Wow! Reading that makes me deeply appreciate the family God has given me... I kept looking, and found on "Web MD" an article that deals with the "holiday family get together" as almost some kind of modern disease when Dr. R. Morgan Griffin wrote:

"There's this idea that holiday gatherings with family are supposed to be joyful and stress-free, ... That's not the case. Family relationships are complicated. But that's doesn't mean that the solution is to skip the holidays entirely." The doctor went on to describe five reasons for the anxiety of family get assemblies: 1) Unhappy memories. Going home for the holidays naturally makes people remember old times, but for you the memories may be more bitter than sweet... 2) Toxic relatives. Holidays can put you in the same room with relatives you avoid the rest of the year... 3) What's changed. The holidays can highlight everything that's changed in your lives — a divorce, a death in the family, a son who's making his first trip back home after starting college...4) What's stayed the same. For others, it's the monotonous sameness of family holiday gatherings that depresses them — the same faces, the same jokes, the same food on the same china plates...5) Lowered defenses. During the holiday season, you're more likely to be stressed out by obligations and errands. It's cold and flu season and your immune system is under assault. It's getting dark earlier each day. You're eating worse, sleeping less, and drinking more. By the time the family gathering rolls around, you're worn out, tense, and fragile. The holiday stress makes it harder to cope with your family than it might be at other times of the year..."

That's right, they must be sick of each other because of low tolerance to the flu. Is he serious? Ah yes, the holiday season...Time to fret, fight and feel terrible. Doesn't America sound like a warm and friendly place these days? Well, our world is filled with struggling families that are trying to keep things together. I shudder to think about it, but it is true... and we need to consider how deep this wound goes, and not gloss over it... Truthfully, I don't want to try to settle the domestic issues of the home in this lesson, but I do want to run at problems of A FAMILY – your church family! Our text deals directly with this critical subject of "life in the fellowship of believers" and offers a sobering truth...

Dispelling Myths about the Gospel: Lessons in Galatians

Key Principle: When the family comes together, we must face the fact that some issues (and some people!) need to be dealt with.

Myth Twelve: Since we are "one in Christ" we all will think the same way.

We are going to look at how we deal with **five different kinds of people**, and the issues they bring to the family gathering in the final chapter of Galatians:

- Each believer needs to deal with **weak brothers** – those who are caught in sin and need release.

- Each believer needs to deal with **self-reliant believers** – those who are deceived into thinking they don't need the rest of the body.

- Each believer needs to deal introspectively and regularly with **his own heart.**

- Each believer needs to deal with the **variety of personalities and gifts** found within the church community – without being "wrung out".

- Each believer needs to deal with **ongoing agitators outside the body** that are poking at the church with biblical truth and gracious outreach until they make it impossible to do so.

The chapter opens with those who have fallen into sinful behaviors, who will need assistance to get back on the path of walking with God. We will call them…

Weaker Brothers: Dealing with the CAUGHT

These are people who asked Jesus to be their Savior, but after a time they found themselves unable to follow through on their walk in some area or behavior. Sometimes it was due to slipping back into a pattern of their old life, and sometimes the slip came because of flaws that were not yet addressed in their character growth as believers. Let's read about them:

Galatians 6:1 Brethren, even if anyone is caught in any trespass, you who are spiritual, restore such a one in a spirit of gentleness; each one looking to yourself, so that you too will not be tempted.

The term "caught" in 6:1 was *prolambanó*, a compound word that paired *pro* "before" and *lambano* "to take." When paired together, they mean in this case "to come upon in advance" as a thief would be discovered or overtaken by an owner of the household. The term "trespass" is *paraptóma*, another compound word that properly meant "a fall beside or near something" but when used figuratively (as in this use) meant "a lapse or deviation" from right behavior as in a sin. We looked at these words to help us truly grasp WHOM Paul was referring to when he wrote. It appears they were people who were discovered in the midst of involvement in something they did not plan to do, but rather fell into. In the strictest sense, they made a choice, but not with great extended intent to do so.

Let's say it this way: **They were CAUGHT in something that seemed to have power over them, and the behavior or action was causing them to SLIP and FALL back into a pattern of sinful behavior.** Wise is the man or woman of God who recognizes how fragile our faithfulness to God truly is! Galatians 6:1 offers five details of the restoration process:

First, the work is distinct. The violator must be a brother or sister in Christ ("brethren"). The address is to believers about believers, and teaches NOTHING about interaction between believers and those who do not follow Christ.

The work is also determined. Both the violator must admit the behavior is NOT God honoring ("trespass") and the responders must agree by Spirit-led and biblical understanding it is a violation ("spiritual"). Nothing is to be gained by putting people who are in sin together with people who do not have the maturity to identify the behavior as a violation of God's Word. This is one of the reasons we need to be careful to be a part of a local church where the *Bible* is carefully studied, and where you have confidence the leadership truly recognizes biblical truth and error. Nothing will do more harm to a person who is caught that to have that person affirmed in their wrong actions because they were with leaders who did not recognize the truth of their behavior!

The work is deliberate. The goal is to bring back to proper use ("restore"). The term "restore" is *katartízō* from *katá*, "according to, down," and *artízō*, "to adjust." Together, the word means to be adjusted back to good working order. The PURPOSE of the gentle work of godly brothers is to get the wayward brother or sister back on track and walking with Jesus.

We must be careful here. It is easy to gracelessly confront someone when he is wrong, because we are annoyed or embarrassed at their behavior, in front of others we care about. That isn't our call. Our Lord instructed brokenness in our hearts toward the caught one, and a goal of restoration. I want to illustrate the idea of restoration if I can…

A few Christmases ago, a twenty-four year old son of Christian parents began a terrible killing spree at the "Youth with A Mission" Headquarters that ended hours later with his injury and subsequent suicide at a second location – the New Life Church in Colorado Springs. Matthew J. Murray was responsible for shooting several people in the church parking lot and in the church building – a spree that left three dead and three wounded. Earlier that day, he had entered the "Youth with A Mission" Headquarters in suburban Denver, shooting four and killing two. The tragedy shook New Life Church that had just started to come out of the painful and very public story about their former nationally known Pastor's sexual sin (that was Ted Haggard). Now they were faced with this terrible tragedy. Sometime after those events, *Christianity Today* published an article that offered a stunning picture of Jesus and restoration...

It seems that after the tragedy, Pastor Brady Boyd, then Senior Minister of New Life Church, called Matthew Murray's parents (the shooter) and asked if they would like to come to New Life and see where 'their son had passed away.' They said they had wanted to, but had refrained from doing so because of their concerns for the church. They were also asked if they would be willing to meet with members of the family who had lost two teenage daughters that morning. They said yes. The same invitation was extended to the victim's family, the Work's. They said yes. After showing the Murrays around the church where the tragic events took place, they met with Mr. and Mrs. Works in Boyd's office. "What happened there in the two hours in my office was the most significant ministry moment I've experienced, maybe in all of my life," Boyd said. When they first entered the office, the two families embraced. They sat, wept, and cried together, Boyd said, for "I don't know how long." Then they prayed together. Later Jeanne Assam [the security guard who shot and wounded Murray before he committed suicide] joined them. When Jeanne, who had undoubtedly saved many lives but had been forced to shoot the Murray's son, walked into the room, "the Murrays embraced her and hugged her and released her from any guilt and remorse. Matthew Murray's dad looked at Jeanne and said, "Please know we're so sorry that you had to do what you did. We're so sorry." The article concluded with these words from Boyd, "We can talk philosophically about repentance and redemption and going forward with God, but what I saw in that room in my office was the greatest testimony of forgiveness and redemption that I have ever seen. It was a testimony that God really can restore and redeem." (Adapted from a message by Pastor Jim Kane, taken from sermoncentral.com)

I recognize the boy wasn't there, and I understand that he wasn't restored. The purpose of the illustration was to highlight the deep emotional nature of restoration. These families were not fractured from one another, but were drawn together at the foot of the Cross. That is the way restoration should look when a CAUGHT ONE is restored as well.

The work is delicate and must be handled with deep sensitivity ("spirit of gentleness"). Did you notice the "spirit" of the work? The word *prautés* is "meekness" (or "gentle strength"). Though it takes STRENGTH to confront sin, it takes GENTLENESS to restore one who has been caught in the snare. That may seem counter-intuitive. Let me suggest a secret: brokenness over sin. If we are truly broken FOR our brother, their correction is for THEM, and not to preserve our reputation, or to indignantly defend Jesus. If we come with broken hearts and a hunger to see the violator restored to a place of blessing – the caught one will know it.

The work is dangerous ("looking to yourself" and "tempted"). There is a danger of smugness that sows the deep seeds of arrogance within those who correct a straying brother – so Paul warned them to be careful!! The spirit of the Pharisee, who stood on the corner and prayed aloud: "Oh Lord, I am glad I am not as that other man!" lives inside us all – and we must be careful to guard our heart.

If the one overtaken in sin is restored, we have added a new joy to the household of God, and removed a cancer that could have spread rapidly. Nothing is served by God's people ignoring sin in the family... nothing! At the same time, there are others that will need to be "dealt with" as well...

Self-reliant Believers: Dealing with the Deceived

There are people who believe they are self-sufficient in Messiah, and do not grow to recognize their responsibility of involving themselves in caring for the needs of others – but they are deceived. Paul wrote:

Galatians 6:2 Bear one another's burdens, and thereby fulfill the law of Christ. 3 For if anyone thinks he is something when he is nothing, he deceives himself.

God placed in every church those who need help. Some are overtaken by a specific sin, and others are simply weakened by living in a sin-sick, fallen world. Look closely at verse two, and you will learn **three important truths about dealing with deceived people in the church:**

The work is planned. Believers are called to SHARE the load of those who are unable to carry it themselves (i.e. "bear one another's burdens"). In truth, God deliberately gives some among us a burden to carry that is quite large, so He can draw together those who are in the body beside them. Often, troubles keep the team together, but there is even a greater benefit. Those who feel "too important" to care for others are exposed as deceived. The greater need is not found in the one who had a burden too large, but in the one who had a deception so hidden. Self-sufficiency is not the mark of following Jesus, sensitivity is.

The work is prescribed: It is a matter of OBEDIENCE, not choice or preference (note the phrase "law of Christ"), particularly because it helps reveal some who have a self-deception based on inordinate confidence ("deceives himself"). We cannot claim we "don't feel called to help each other" because we are commanded to do so.

The work is piercing: It calls for people who are involved in the process to look honestly and deeply within ("deceives himself"). The person under restoration dare not think they can do this without help – because pride is part of the sin formula. The same is true of those who think they are too good to get their hands dirty.

Here, though, is the really "tricky part" of load bearing. **When am I ENABLING another, as opposed to properly helping them**

with their load? The context is someone who is CAUGHT in a sinful behavior (6:1), or to keep the imagery solid, TRAPPED under a load. The load is clearly sinful behavior, and it is something both THE TRAPPED ONE and the RESCUERS see as a collapse that can and must be moved. The load is removed when the sin has been set aside.

Let me say it this way: Johnnie and Suzie met and were married. Johnnie grew up in church, but he wasn't a Christian in the *Bible* sense of asking Jesus to live and reign in Him. Suzie was largely unchurched, and also had made no commitment to Christ. Johnnie was deeply involved with pornography since he was a young man, and Suzie had little resistance to his participation, since she really didn't see this as a problem. Johnnie and Suzie were both befriended by a new couple that moved in next door. They were impressed with this couple, and really appreciated their humor, and their integrity. In time, Johnnie and Suzie were led to Jesus by their friends. For a while, Johnnie set aside his pornography because his excitement in his Christian life helped him to really enjoy Suzie in new and deep ways – as they both grew in their walk with God and each other. They connected now on a level neither could quite understand. About that time, Johnnie's work situation changed. He was moved from his day shift to an all night shift schedule. His world was turned upside down. Suzie worked days, he worked nights – life got strained. Time apart led him to feeling unattached again – and the porn became his coping mechanism. Suzie came home early one day and discovered Johnnie feeding the old habit again. She was crushed! She went to some of her believing friends and asked for help – and two guys came to see Johnnie. They didn't shake their finger at him – they understood the problem and really tried to help get Johnnie out from under the load of guilt and the threatening cracks to his marriage. They were sensitive to his feelings, but they still directed him to get out from under the load. If Johnnie chose to admit the problem, and turn from it – the load was lifted. If he chose to refuse to eliminate it from his life – and he continued to do the wrong thing, he was not restored. If he decides to "DO IT ALL BY HIMSELF" – pushing away the help of others, he will likely overestimate his own strengths and abilities to cope with his desires. In any case, he cannot claim victim status and say, "They don't really care about me!" if he refused to turn from the sinful practice. Bearing any burden that comes directly from a choice to remain in sin would be sharing in that sin and enabling it.

Perhaps one of the hardest people in the church to deal with is the person inside our own skin...

My Heart: Dealing with Myself

Verse four seems to continue the look within that was opened in verse three with the idea of "deceives himself." One problem we may have is self-deception in the area of OVERINFLATED EGO – but that isn't the only self-deception we must guard against. A second one may be found in CONSTANT COMPARISON. Instead of heeding the Word in our own lives, we can easily become numb to our own walk and focus on the walk of others around us.

Some believers come to church with the wrong tool in their hand. It is easy to get used to coming to church with a shovel, hearing truth and passing it out to people without pulling it toward us (as with a rake). We hear something, and before we even allow ourselves to apply it, we are tossing it to someone we believe needed to hear it more!

Paul charged the Galatian believers to self-examination...

Galatians 6:4 But each one must examine his own work, and then he will have reason for boasting in regard to himself alone, and not in regard to another. 5 For each one will bear his own load.

This self-examination is a productive work. In dealing with another rightly, I must inspect myself closely. God not only provided the one who was over-burdened to draw us together, but to make us see our own frailty and weakness, and keep us seeing ourselves clearly.

The nineteenth century theologian and Pastor, Albert Barnes' made this note on Galatians 6:4-5: The man who forms an improper estimate of his own character will be sure to be disappointed. The man who examines himself, and who forms no extravagant expectation in regard to what is due to himself, will be appropriately rewarded, and will be made happy. ... Compare Proverbs 14:14; "A good man shall be satisfied from himself." The sentiment is, that ... In an approving conscience; in the evidence of the favor of God; in an honest effort to lead a pure and holy life, he will have happiness. The source of his joys will be within; and he will not be dependent, as the man of ambition, and the man who thinks of himself more highly than he ought, will, on the favors of a capricious multitude, and on the breath of popular applause.

Let's be clear about what Paul is calling for. Paul told the Galatians NOT to examine another without examining themselves – just as Jesus told His followers to remove the LOG from their own eye before judging another. Yet, that was not the END of the saying. The Apostle went on to make clear to the Galatians that they SHOULD then turn to deal with erring believers, while seeking to keep their own house in order. The modern believer may draw the conclusion that identifying sin in another is "judging another" – and conclude it is intrinsically wrong to do so. Yet, that is not what the Bible truly teaches. On close inspection, such judgments ARE to be made, if we are to fulfill our call to show practical love. We MUST judge our own actions, but we are also called to clearly call sin what it is in BOTH self and others on the way to attempting to rescue a fallen brother. We will not boldly attempt any such rescue to which we were called if we fail to recognize the peril to the life of the one caught in sin. If we allow another to continue in sin's trap without attempting rescue because we thought we "didn't have the right to judge their behavior," we will fail to follow all the commands related to attempting restoration of the ensnared. That gently pushes us to dealing with others in the family of believers...

Dealing with my believing family

Galatians 6:6 The one who is taught the word is to share all good things with the one who teaches him. 7 Do not be deceived, God is not mocked; for whatever a man sows, this he will also reap. 8 For the one who sows to his own flesh will from the flesh reap corruption, but the one who sows to the Spirit will from the Spirit reap eternal life. 9 Let us not lose heart in doing good, for in due time we will reap if we do not grow weary. 10 So then, while we have opportunity, let us do good to all people, and especially to those who are of the household of the faith.

First, Paul made it clear that believers who were growing were to "share all good things" with those who were sowing spiritual truth into their lives. In the first century when this command was written, it may have been hard for some in the house-church of the period to recognize the work involved in equipping and training believers by elders who were bi-vocational (working another job all day). Some believers were slaves and had little to offer their teaching elder to compensate for the extra hours of work to train them in Christ. What they COULD offer, and what they were TOLD to offer, included more than just support. It included encouragement. It included sharing with their teacher the lessons God was using in their lives. The "all good things" isn't just money – it includes a host of other encouragements as well.

Second, in the middle of the point about sharing good things, Paul reminded the Galatians of a truth believers often forget: we will reap what we sow. If we invest hours in fleshly pursuits, but neglect the pursuit of knowing God's Word – we will not be transformed by the renewing of our minds. We will be "pressed into the mold of the world." Tragically, I see many believers who are harming the cause of Christ in the public square because they know Him, but not His teaching. They have spent hours on secular education, but have been contented with minutes a week in God's Word. They have sown the principles of a world that is fading away, but not learned of the world that is emerging after. They have a conscience that has been seared and tailored to modernity, but not transformed by Christ. Rather than offer help to the church, they often become those who cause most of the problems – They don't see SIN as SIN – because they have learned the world's fluctuation definition of "right" and "wrong," "fair" and "unfair," "just" and "unjust."

These are the "friends" on Facebook who offer pronouncements like, "Jesus never spoke out on things like abortion or same-sex marriage. The church must be off base for spending time on these things." They mean well, but they **haven't studied well.** They forgot that Jesus was the same Lord as the One at Sinai, or that He is "the expressed image of God Himself." They forgot that when Jesus lived, the Law took care of such things. The word for those involved in such a "marriage" was "stoned" outside the city gate. They forget that when Paul, who lived in the Roman world outside the parameters of the standard of God's Torah Law encountered these ideas, had very stern judgments concerning them, commanding people not to allow them a meal among them (1 Corinthians 5-6). Believers who sow worldly learning harm the spread of the Word's transformational power.

Third, because the world buffets against the spirit and because even some of the believers refuse to be careful to

sow in the spirit by learning the Word – walking with Jesus in the context of the body can become exhausting. Paul told those who were tired not to allow themselves to "lose heart" in well doing. Remember, we don't own the world – we just work for the One Who does. People who fail to walk with Christ aren't primarily failing US – they are failing the Master. We should pull from within LOVE not ANGER. We should answer their failure by PRAYER for them, and while keeping our house in order, careful outreach to them. Yet, there will be another group we must keep a steady eye upon...

Dealing with Agitators (from outside the body)

The phrase we use for agitators is often "playing the devil's advocate" – and that is a good terminology. The problem is, that many of us don't see why that is a problem any longer. We are very comfortable listening to the devil's argument up close. Paul knew them. The agitators were attending the small house church fellowships in Galatia, and diverting attention from the balanced teaching of God's Word. He wrote:

Galatians 6:11 See with what large letters I am writing to you with my own hand. 12 Those who desire to make a good showing in the flesh try to compel you to be circumcised, simply so that they will not be persecuted for the cross of Christ. 13 For those who are circumcised do not even keep the Law themselves, but they desire to have you circumcised so that they may boast in your flesh. 14 But may it never be that I would boast, except in the cross of our Lord Jesus Christ, through which the world has been crucified to me, and I to the world. 15 For neither is circumcision anything, nor uncircumcision, but a new creation. 16 And those who will walk by this rule, peace and mercy be upon them, and upon the Israel of God. 17 From now on let no one cause trouble for me, for I bear on my body the brand-marks of Jesus.

Paul ended the letter with a few warnings about **two kinds of agitations** that have popped up in the church since its inception. The enemy uses these all the time, and we need to help young believers sort out these sneaky approaches to pull them away…

The first is "Agitation by confusion". Paul made sure they knew HE wrote the letter, at least at the end of the scroll where it would show he personally endorsed the contents. It appears that some agitators had already spread a "false scroll" in Corinth, and Paul identified this trick and worked to thwart it. Today we see this same method – with young or poorly taught believers being "hacked" by confusion-geared arguments.

Worldviews are shaped in the education system that is increasingly being reworked at the foundational level to retrain the thinking of our youth. Much of the post 1960 re-engineering of American culture began as social experimentation in a classroom.

Here is a simple example. Train young people to think this way: "Those who oppose sanctioning under law the lifestyle choices of other people are bigots" - and you will produce a generation that believes it is intrinsically wrong to make value judgments about behaviors in the public square. Relativism will be enshrined in their thinking. When they grow up, as voters, they will believe that no one has the right to judge any lifestyle choices and behaviors of another – and their state will be forced to mandate all choices as equal under the law. They will fail to understand that such judgments are necessary to operate a stable republic and stop a cultural decline. They will lack the long-term understanding to know that routinely licensing behaviors that are harmful to the whole of the community will only cause the community to lose the bonds that held it together. The end is the death of the connected community itself. In one generation, they will hail the rise of the un-bonded "test tube baby" without regard to the crying young people that filled Oprah's set in search of their parents and their biological identity a generation later... They will fail to think long term about the outcomes of social experimentation.

Closer to the training in the Scriptures, sometimes unsuspecting and young believers are sucked into the internet discussions that offer a distilled version of two thousand years of attacks against the *Bible*. They are tugged to conclude that the *Bible* has "many interpretations" as if God was somehow unclear. They don't recognize that most all of the attacks on the *Bible* now are repeats of earlier attacks over the centuries that were long ago answered. Previous generations of Christians took time to learn the Bible well at an early age in their faith and those attacks didn't gain such ground as they do now. Today the church is filled with the legions of the untaught and retrained thinkers, as susceptible to attack as the weakened body is to infection. While cults will introduce "another testament of Jesus Christ," others will introduce young Christians to the "lost *Bible* books", like the *Nag Hammadi Documents*, etc. This is an old ploy of our enemy – to deceive with false words and water down true words. Paul shot back in 6:11 by making sure they knew what was authentic – because he spotted the attack. May we be so diligent!

The second is "Agitation by Controlling Interests". Paul made clear the attempts at abuse of those who wanted to gain control of the fledgling house church groups that were following Jesus. He made clear (cp. 6:12) how to recognize them – "those who... compel you to be circumcised", because that was THEIR ISSUE. Paul explained their real purpose – to boast in their control over you.

Paul warned that Judaizers wanted to control the believers. Today, I would suggest that American political forces have done this with Christendom in our country. The right hearkens to the evangelical movement, while the left beckons the liberal movement. Neither political framework, of itself, cares a whit for the Christ presented in the Bible, and the spread of the Gospel. Each are using religion to prop up their point of view and gain followers, and to keep saints enraged by the other side's abuses. Their ultimate angle is control... I am not suggesting that each side doesn't have some positive moral concepts within their framework – quite the opposite. The right emphasizes responsibility (and that is needed) while the left reminds the citizenry of the less fortunate and needy (another biblically important concern). My point is this: Christians must not put our trust in the bonds forged between political entities and Christianity – they are short lived and constantly shifting. We mustn't look for media outlets to truly defend Jesus – they will only do so if the ratings and income make that a good thing for them to do in the short term. The world and its organizations are not where Christian energies should peak – but rather they should invest appropriate energy in the public issues only after undergirding themselves in the spiritual disciplines of prayer, study, quiet reflection and engaging in the practical neighborly help of those in need.

These are heavy words and important teachings that help us deal with others in the church family. At the same time, they can lead us to a negative feeling about life – and that is not what Paul desired, nor what the Spirit wants. Let's end our study with the same sense that Paul did... a spirit of grace and a trust in God's plan. He ended with Jesus – not simply with the believer! He wrote a simple ending sentence to the Galatian believers:

Galatians 6:18: The grace of our Lord Jesus Christ be with your spirit, brethren. Amen.

Paul ended with words of God's grace – of the undeserved favor of Jesus Christ to those of us who have experienced the depth of His love! The message of Christ is not the prevue of a select few professional ministers – it never has been! The qualification for effectiveness in helping the body stand well is to be in love with the Savior, and follow His directions. I close with a simple illustration of that very truth from American history:

In 1857 there was a 46-year-old man named Jeremiah Lamphere who lived in New York City. Jeremiah loved the Lord tremendously, but he didn't feel that he could do much for the Lord until he began to feel a burden for the lost and accepted an invitation from his church to be an inner city missionary. So, in July of 1857, he started walking up and down the streets of New York passing out tracts and talking to people about Jesus, but he wasn't having any success. Then God put it on his heart to try prayer. He printed up a bunch of tracts, and he passed them out to anyone and everyone he met. He invited anyone who wanted to come to the 3rd floor of the Old North Dutch Reformed Church on Fulton St. in New York City from 12 to 1 on Wednesday to pray. He passed out hundreds and hundreds of fliers and put up posters everywhere he could. Wednesday came and at noon nobody showed up. Jeremiah got on his knees and started praying. For 30 minutes, he prayed by himself when finally five other people walked in. The next week 20 people came. The next week between 30 and 40 people came. They then decided to meet every day from 12:00 to 1:00 to pray for the city. Before long a few ministers started coming and they said, "We need to start this at our churches." Within six months there were over 5000 prayer groups meeting every day in N.Y. Soon the word spread all over the country. Prayer meetings were started in Philadelphia, Detroit, and Washington D.C. In fact, President Franklin Pierce started going almost every day to a noonday prayer meeting. By 1859, some 15,000 cities in America were having downtown prayer meetings every day at noon, and thousands were brought to Christ. The great thing about this revival is that there is not a famous preacher associated with it. It was all started by one man wanting to pray. People have been seeking God, and seeking a relationship with God through Jesus Christ for centuries. (From a sermon by Rich Anderson, *Seeking the Face of Jesus Christ,* 2/18/2011)

Every believer has a Savior, His Spirit, a set of gifts and a calling to serve the Master well. We also have a family in Christ, for better or worse! We must remember...

When the family comes together, we must face the fact that some issues (and some people!) need to be dealt with.

Other volumes in the series through the Bible are available through amazon.com and can be found by searching for:

"Dr. Randall D. Smith"

Free teaching resources are also available at:

www.randalldsmith.com

www.ingramcontent.com/pod-product-compliance
Lightning Source LLC
Chambersburg PA
CBHW060524030426
42337CB00015B/1992